DIESTERWEGS
NEUSPRACHLICHE
BIBLIOTHEK

Thomas L. Friedman

The World Is Flat

Excerpts and key supplementary texts

edited and annotated
by Styles Sass

DIESTERWEG

Druck A[1] / Jahr 2012
Alle Drucke der Serie A sind im Unterricht parallel verwendbar.

Redaktion: Rudolph F. Rau, Schorndorf
Umschlagfoto: Gerd Altmann © Pixelio.de
Umschlagkonzeption: Blum Design und Kommunikation, Hamburg
Herstellung und Umschlagrealisation: Harald Thumser, Frankfurt
Satz: Stahringer Satz GmbH, Grünberg
Druck und Bindung: westermann druck GmbH, Braunschweig

ISBN 978-3-425-04810-3

Table of Contents

Introduction 5

Thomas L. Friedman
The World is Flat 10

Chapter 1 11
Friedman's 10 Flatteners 30

Chapter 2 32
Flattener # 1 32
Flattener # 5 39
Flattener # 7 50
Flattener # 9 66

Chapter 12 76

Fareed Zakaria
The Rise of the Rest 88

Muhammad Yunus
Creating a World Without Poverty 105

Richard Florida
The Rise of the Creative Class 116

Francis Fukuyama
The End of History? 133

Joseph E. Stiglitz
Making Globalization Work 154

Recommended Reading. 158

If you want to see how the traffic is moving, come with me to the FedEx central hub at Memphis International Airport. Things really begin to hum around 11:00 P.M., when 160 airplanes from all over the world begin to converge on this field. If you go to the observation deck at the top of the tower, you get a 360 degree view of the night sky, and you can see points of light coming from all directions. At this hour there is no other air traffic. All the planes are FedEx, and they will land between now and 1:00 A.M. Once on the ground it takes a half hour to unload everything from Dell computers to legal documents to tennis racquets on a big, dumb conveyor that dumps it all into one big bin. The "sort" combines the lowest technology with the highest. At the bin, every package is turned over and sent to the scanner by teams of people who pull and haul all those boxes. Once scanned, the packages go on to smart conveyors that automatically drop them at the right bin for reloading and onward shipment. By 3:00 A.M., all the planes are back in the air and the packages will reach their recipients by 11:00 A.M.[1]

Clyde Prestowitz

[1] Clyde Prestowitz, *Three Billion New Capitalists: the Great Shift of Wealth and Power to the East*, New York: Basic Books, 2005, 36

Introduction

I am not an Athenian or a Greek, but a citizen of the world.

Socrates[1] *(470 to 399 B.C.)*

Images of the earth like the one on the cover of this book have become so commonplace that it is difficult for us to understand how it must have felt when, for the first time in history, people saw photographs of our planet floating out in space. A by-product of the Apollo 8 mission in 1968, many authors credit such pictures as the source of a major shift in how humans perceive both themselves and the world around them – the growth of the environmental movement being one example of this.[2] While the quotation from Socrates shows that there have always been individuals who were able to think beyond arbitrary[3] geo-political borders and the identities they imply, it is the scale of this recent shift towards a global consciousness which makes it so significant.

This shift is mainly due to the fact that, throughout the course of our daily lives, we repeatedly experience just how interconnected the world has become. Here one can mention the instantaneous[4] news reports we receive from around the globe, the imported products we buy, the diverse locations to which we travel for business or vacation, the increasingly multi-cultural demographics of our societies, the growing number of jobs that have international dimensions to them, or the obvious fact that you are studying this particular language. Contrary to the semi-conscious notion[5] we often harbor[6] that globalization is something which is happening "out there," in reality, globalization is, well, global. To take the last example, we can see how this process is affecting education in regard to both what we learn and how we learn it. Consider the fact that,

[1] Socrates ['sɒkrəti:z]
[2] Steve Connor, "Forty Years Since the First Picture of Earth from Space," *The Independent*, January 10, 2009, http://www.independent.co.uk/news/science/forty-years-since-the-first-picture-of-earth-from-space-1297569.html
[3] arbitrary: random
[4] instantaneously: at the same moment they are happening
[5] notion: idea
[6] to harbor: to keep within yourself

in order to find out more about the ideology of "cosmopolitanism," you might turn to an Internet search engine, or to look up the definition of the word "disingenuous," as well as listen to a native speaker's recorded pronunciation of it, you can use an on-line dictionary. In both cases, your electronic inquiry[7] will literally travel around the globe and back within seconds, thus giving new meaning to the idea of having the world at your fingertips.

However, it should be stressed[8] at the outset that globalization is not something new. People around the world have always shown an insatiable[9] curiosity about what their "neighbors" were up to – and gone to amazing lengths to find out! Indeed, there is a long history of intercultural exchange. An interesting example of this desire to learn from others, which is evidenced[10] throughout these texts, is the ongoing intellectual dialogue between Germany and the United States. Thus, although there are certainly differences of opinion when it comes to evaluating the consequences of globalization, no one doubts that it has been taking place over the past several centuries, or that its pace[11] has accelerated[12] dramatically over the past few decades. While that might seem obvious, it is still fascinating to look closely at the mechanisms that have brought this situation about, as well as to consider the impact it is having on our lives.

Of course, the world is not really flat, nor did Thomas Friedman mean it that way. As he admits, his title was a way of portraying how dramatically the playing field is being leveled by new technologies that empower individuals, and thus increase competition around the globe. To go back to our example of education, anyone with access[13] to a computer can look up "cosmopolitanism," and "disingenuous," just as easily as you. Muhamad Yunus sees such developments as extremely positive, arguing that they provide opportunities for poorer countries to leapfrog[14] over intermediate stages of development and thus modernize more quickly than anyone could have foreseen. Fareed Zakaria agrees, claiming that this shift in power should not be seen as the decline of the West, but the

---

[7] inquiry: question
[8] to stress: to emphasize
[9] insatiable [ɪnˈseɪʃəbl]: unable to get enough of something
[10] to evidence: to show proof of s.th.
[11] pace: speed
[12] to accelerate: to speed up
[13] access: the possibility to use s.th.
[14] to leapfrog: to make great and rapid progress in a short time, as in the children's game of the same name

"rise of the rest" – the stability it adds to the entire system being something from which we all benefit. Where an author like Joseph Stieglitz disagrees is the extent to which this "flattening," or increase in the equality of opportunity, has taken place. With that in mind, it is more accurate to say that there is a longer process of flattening which has been taking place, rather than a final end-state which has been reached.

Naturally, this flattening also has its down sides. Many jobs have been moved to places where people and natural resources can be exploited for quick profits while, at the same time, income disparity[15] within most nations continues to rise. Population growth and economic development are putting enormous strains on the environment while, relatedly, dangerous diseases can spread further and more rapidly due to our increased mobility. Wealthier nations are experiencing an influx of immigrants from less affluent[16] countries who are willing to work for lower wages, and thus driving down the prices people are willing to pay for their goods and services. The interdependence of markets makes each nation susceptible[17] to the volatilities[18] of the world economy, while political instabilities, natural disasters, and terrorism, all have ramifications[19] far beyond the isolated locations where they occur. For many people it is negative examples like these that have become the face of globalization, and which cause them to either distrust or reject it. This skeptical view seems to be confirmed by even a quick glance through the daily papers, which are filled with troubling news from around the globe.

Without downplaying[20] the gravity[21] of these problems, it must also be said that due to the media's tendency to report dramatic or negative news, we often form a skewed[22] and oversimplified view of the world – losing a sense of proportion against which such events need to be measured. Here it is important to make the distinction between smaller, isolated events that receive a lot of attention, and the long term trends which are often so big as to escape our notice. A good example of this phenomenon is the idea of companies moving to some developing country for reasons of cheap labor. What is often forgotten is that as the standard of living in a country rises, so too do the wages which need to be paid. When taken

[15] disparity: inequality
[16] affluent: with a high standard of living
[17] susceptible [səˈseptəbl]: capable of being influenced by s.th.
[18] volatilities: changes
[19] ramifications: effects
[20] to downplay: to make less important
[21] gravity: seriousness
[22] skewed [skjuːd]: biased

alongside productivity levels, quality controls, transportation costs, and delivery times, these higher wages make future mass investment less attractive, thus leading to a more general flattening of competitive advantage around the globe.

In part, it is this increased competition which is demanding ever more creativity in the workplace – a quality which Richard Florida argues is transforming major aspects of our societies. In fact, many of the authors collected here see us moving towards a kind of cosmopolitan Meritocracy, where social rewards will not be distributed on the basis of ethnicity, gender, class, or personal preferences of religion or sexual orientation, but simply on who can achieve the best results. Such changes in attitude seem to be confirmed by the 2008 presidential election, when we remember that, even a mere twenty years ago, it would have been unthinkable that an African American who had lived most of his life outside the continental United States, and had a name like Barack Hussein Obama, could ever be elected to the highest office of the land. Indeed, a quick look over the names of the authors included in this book reveals[23] the extent to which ethnic diversity has become a common facet of our global society.

In addition, an overly critical stance towards globalization is disingenuous if we do not acknowledge all its benefits which we now take for granted. It is the depth and breadth of these benefits which make it unlikely that any of us would really choose to go back to a pre-globalized world. Indeed, it is a curious quality of technological progress that once we have something which makes our lives more convenient[24] or efficient, it is difficult to remember how we ever survived without it. Often, however, this does not stop us from complaining about the side effects or consequences of these improvements. To take the most obvious example, while few would be willing to give up their cell phones, few want to live near the transmission masts which are necessary for them to function. This tension between our desires and their costs reminds one of Walter Kelly's[25] famous slogan for the first-ever Earth Day celebration in 1970: "We have met the enemy and he is us."

While the difficulties accompanying[26] globalization should certainly not be underestimated,[27] nor should the possibilities they represent, for

[23] to reveal: to show
[24] convenient [kən'vi:niənt]: comfortable
[25] Walter Kelly (1913–1973): American political cartoonist
[26] to accompany: to go along with
[27] to underestimate: to evaluate as less than s.th. really is

it is precisely qualities like creativity, cooperation, pragmatism, compassion, and intellectual honesty, which the solutions to these challenges will demand. From past and present examples, we know that progress, leading to a better future, is possible. Indeed, one of the noticeable effects of globalization is the spread of democratic and liberal values to all corners of the earth. Francis Fukuyama goes as far as to argue that we have reached the end of a historic struggle between competing ideologies – the human and natural resources which this struggle consumed now being freed up to improve the lives of people around the world.

It is, of course, always risky to guess at the significance of events when one is in the middle of them and lacking any historical perspective. In his diary entry of July 4th, 1776, King George III wrote, "Nothing important happened today." While it must be said that he was not aware that the United States had just declared their independence from England when he wrote those words, there is reason to believe that, even if he had been, his world view based on British dominance would have remained unshakable.

In the same way, it is difficult for us to understand and evaluate the changes that have been sweeping over our world in the last thirty years. But if there is one main idea that emerges from these texts it is that, more than anything, globalization is about you – and, by extension, each of us. For we are all becoming citizens of our commonly shared planet, with all the exciting opportunities and worrisome challenges that situation carries with it. It is up to us to create a system of global order which is respectful toward people around the world and the environment upon which we all depend. Therefore, I urge you to read the texts in this book carefully and reflect on them critically, for they represent some of the most important thinking on the mechanisms and implications of globalization. It is, after all, this process and the bundle of issues connected to it that will continue to shape our flattening world for decades to come.

Styles Sass 2011

Thomas L. Friedman was born in Minneapolis, Minnesota in 1953. He graduated summa cum laude in 1975 from Brandeis University with a degree in Mediterranean studies, and later received an M. Phil. Degree in modern Middle East studies from Oxford University. He began his journalism career in London and eventually began writing for the *New York Times*, where has won three Pulitzer Prizes for his work. He was the author of three previous bestsellers and in 2005 he published his fourth book, originally titled, *The World Is Flat: A Brief History of the Twenty-first Century*. It became a #1 *New York Times* bestseller, received the inaugural Financial Times/Goldman Sachs Business Book of the Year Award, and has sold more than 4 million copies in thirty-seven languages. He and his wife live in Bethesda, Maryland and have two daughters.

In the excerpts collected here, Friedman begins by describing how his experiences in international reporting led him to view the world as "flat." After describing the historical development of globalization, he goes on to describe some of the mechanisms by which it has been pushed to its current level – which he terms "3.0." In a newly added chapter, Friedman also addresses the issue of cultural homogenization, arguing that just the opposite is taking place; namely, the "globalization of the local." You can watch part of a lecture by Thomas Friedman at: http://www.youtube.com/watch?v=oM2BguxRSyY.

The World is Flat[1] (Excerpts)

by Thomas L. Friedman

Chapter 1: While I Was Sleeping

No one ever gave me directions like this on a golf course before: "Aim at either Microsoft or IBM." I was standing on the first tee[2] at the KGA Golf Club in downtown Bangalore, in southern India, when my playing partner pointed at two shiny glass-and-steel buildings off in the distance, just behind the first green. The Goldman Sachs building wasn't done yet; otherwise he could have pointed that out as well and made it a threesome. HP and Texas Instruments had their offices on the back nine,[3] along the tenth hole. That wasn't all. The tee markers were from Epson, the printer company, and one of our caddies was wearing a hat from 3M. Outside, some of the traffic signs were also sponsored by Texas Instruments, and the Pizza Hut billboard on the way over showed a steaming pizza, under the headline "Gigabites of Taste!"

No, this definitely wasn't Kansas.[4] It didn't even seem like India. Was this the New World, the Old World, or the Next World?

I had come to Bangalore, India's Silicon Valley, on my own Columbus-like journey of exploration. Columbus sailed with the *Niña*, the *Pinta*, and the *Santa Maria* in an effort to discover a shorter, more direct route to India by heading west, across the Atlantic, on what he presumed to be an open sea route to the East Indies – rather than going south and east around Africa, as Portuguese explorers of his day were trying to do. India and the magical Spice Islands of the East were famed at the time for their gold, pearls, gems, and silk – a source of untold riches. Finding this shortcut by sea to India, at a time when the Muslim powers of the day had blocked the overland routes from Europe, was a way for both Columbus and the Spanish monarchy to become wealthy and powerful. When Columbus set sail, he apparently assumed the earth was round,

[1] Thomas L. Friedman, *The World is Flat: The Globalized World in the Twenty-First Century*, New York: Penguin, 2006, 3–11, 40–50, 51–59, 126–136, 151–166, 177–185, 477–488

[2] tee (golf): the place from which one begins each hole

[3] back nine: holes 10 through 18 on a golf course

[4] wasn't Kansas: play on a line spoken by the main character in the film *The Wizard of Oz*, signifying that one is in a strange and unfamiliar place

which was why he was convinced that he could get to India by going west. He miscalculated the distance, though. He thought the earth was a smaller sphere than it is. He also did not anticipate running into a landmass before he reached the East Indies. Nevertheless, he called the aboriginal peoples he encountered in the new world "Indians." Returning home, though, Columbus was able to tell his patrons,[5] King Ferdinand and Queen Isabella, that although he never did find India, he could confirm that the world was indeed round.

I set out for India by going due east, via Frankfurt. I had Lufthansa business class. I knew exactly which direction I was going thanks to the GPS map displayed on the screen that popped out of the armrest of my airline seat. I landed safely and on schedule. I too encountered people called Indians. I too was searching for India's riches. Columbus was searching for hardware – precious metals, silk, and spices – the sources of wealth in his day. I was searching for software, brainpower, complex algorithms, knowledge workers, call centers, transmission protocols,[6] breakthroughs in optical engineering – the sources of wealth in our day.

Columbus was happy to make the Indians he met his slaves, a pool of free manual labor.[7] I just wanted to understand why the Indians I met were taking our work, why they had become such an important pool for the outsourcing of service and information technology work from America and other industrialized countries. Columbus had more than one hundred men on his three ships; I had a small crew[8] from the Discovery Times channel[9] that fit comfortably into two banged-up[10] vans, with Indian drivers who drove barefoot. When I set sail, so to speak, I too assumed that the world was round, but what I encountered in the real India profoundly shook my faith in that notion. Columbus accidentally ran into America but thought he had discovered part of India. I actually found India and thought many of the people I met there were Americans. Some had actually taken American names, and others were doing great imitations of American accents at call centers and American business techniques at software labs.

[5] patron: person providing financial support
[6] protocol (IT): rules that determine how data is sent
[7] manual labor: physical work
[8] crew [kru:] (here): technicians helping to film the documentary for the television channel
[9] Discovery Time channel: commercial information channel in the USA, now called Investigation Discovery
[10] banged up (colloquial): dented (*mit Beulen*)

Columbus reported to his king and queen that the world was round, and he went down in history as the man who first made this discovery. I returned home and shared my discovery only with my wife, and only in a whisper.

"Honey,"[11] I confided, "I think the world is flat."

How did I come to this conclusion? I guess you could say it all started in Nandan Nilekani's conference room at Infosys Technologies Limited. Infosys is one of the jewels of the Indian information technology world, and Nilekani, the company's CEO, is one of the most thoughtful and respected captains of Indian industry. I drove with the Discovery Times crew out to the Infosys campus, about forty minutes from the heart of Bangalore, to tour the facility and interview Nilekani. The Infosys campus is reached by a pockmarked road,[12] with sacred cows,[13] horse-drawn carts, and motorized rickshaws all jostling[14] alongside our vans. Once you enter the gates of Infosys, though, you are in a different world. A massive resort-size swimming pool nestles[15] amid boulders and manicured lawns, adjacent to a huge putting green.[16] There are multiple restaurants and a fabulous health club. Glass-and-steel buildings seem to sprout up like weeds each week. In some of those buildings, Infosys employees are writing specific software programs for American or European companies; in others, they are running the back rooms of major American – and European-based multinationals – everything from computer maintenance to specific research projects to answering customer calls routed there from all over the world. Security is tight, cameras monitor the doors, and if you are working for American Express, you cannot get into the building that is managing services and research for General Electric. Young Indian engineers, men and women, walk briskly from building to building, dangling ID badges.[17] One looked like he could do my taxes. Another looked like she could take my computer apart. And a third looked like she designed it!

After sitting for an interview, Nilekani gave our TV crew a tour of Infosys's global conferencing center – ground zero[18] of the Indian out-

[11] honey (colloquial): term for a loved one
[12] pockmarked road: one with holes in it
[13] sacred cows: reference to the Hindu religion's ban on slaughtering cows
[14] to jostle: (here): to struggle to get ahead of the others
[15] to nestle ['nesl]: to lie in a protected place
[16] putting ['pʌtɪŋ] green (golf): a place to practice the final shots of each hole when the ball is knocked into the cup
[17] ID badges: identification badges
[18] ground zero: the center

sourcing industry. It was a cavernous wood-paneled room that looked like a tiered[19] classroom from an Ivy League law school. On one end was a massive wall-size screen and overhead there were cameras in the ceiling for teleconferencing. "So this is our conference room, probably the largest screen in Asia – this is forty digital screens [put together]," Nilekani explained proudly, pointing to the biggest flat-screen TV I had ever seen. Infosys, he said, can hold a virtual meeting of the key players from its entire global supply chain[20] for any project at any time on that supersize screen. So their American designers could be on the screen speaking with their Indian software writers and their Asian manufacturers all at once. "We could be sitting here, somebody from New York, London, Boston, San Francisco, all live. And maybe the implementation is in Singapore, so the Singapore person could also be live here ... That's globalization," said Nilekani. Above the screen there were eight clocks that pretty well summed up the Infosys workday: 24/7/365.[21] The clocks were labeled US West, US East, GMT,[22] India, Singapore, Hong Kong, Japan, Australia.

"Outsourcing is just one dimension of a much more fundamental thing happening today in the world," Nilekani explained. "What happened over the last [few] years is that there was a massive investment in technology, especially in the bubble era,[23] when hundreds of millions of dollars were invested in putting broadband connectivity around the world, undersea cables, all those things." At the same time, he added, computers became cheaper and dispersed all over the world, and there was an explosion of software-e-mail, search engines like Google, and proprietary software[24] that can chop up any piece of work and send one part to Boston, one part to Bangalore, and one part to Beijing, making it easy for anyone to do remote development. When all of these things suddenly came together around 2000, added Nilekani, they "created a platform where intellectual work, intellectual capital, could be delivered from anywhere. It could be disaggregated,[25] delivered, distributed, produced, and put back together again – and this gave a whole new degree of freedom to the way we do work, especially work of an intellectual

[19] tiered: having ascending levels
[20] supply chain: the way of organizing everything necessary to get a product from the producer to the customer
[21] 24/7/365: 24 hours a day, 7 days a week, 365 days a year
[22] GMT: Greenwich ['grenɪtʃ] Mean Time
[23] bubble era: the era of the "new economy" at the beginning of the 21st century that then collapsed
[24] proprietary software: software that is copyrighted
[25] to disaggregate: to separate into parts

nature ... And what you are seeing in Bangalore today is really the culmination[26] of all these things coming together."

We were sitting on the couch outside Nilekani's office, waiting for the TV crew to set up its cameras. At one point, summing up the implications of all this, Nilekani uttered a phrase that rang in my ear. He said to me, "Tom, the playing field is being leveled." He meant that countries like India are now able to compete for global knowledge work as never before – and that America had better get ready for this. America was going to be challenged, but, he insisted, the challenge would be good for America because we are always at our best when we are being challenged. As I left the Infosys campus that evening and bounced along the road back to Bangalore, I kept chewing on that phrase: "The playing field is being leveled."

What Nandan is saying, I thought to myself, is that the playing field is being flattened ... Flattened? Flattened? I rolled that word around in my head for a while and then, in the chemical way that these things happen, it just popped out: My God, he's telling me the world is flat!

Here I was in Bangalore – more than five hundred years after Columbus sailed over the horizon, using the rudimentary navigational technologies of his day, and returned safely to prove definitively that the world was round – and one of India's smartest engineers, trained at his country's top technical institute and backed by the most modern technologies of his day, was essentially[27] telling me that the world was *flat* – as flat as that screen on which he can host a meeting of his whole global supply chain. Even more interesting, he was citing this development as a good thing, as a new milestone in human progress and a great opportunity for India and the world – the fact that we had made our world flat!

In the back of that van, I scribbled down[28] four words in my notebook: "The world is flat." As soon as I wrote them, I realized that this was the underlying[29] message of everything that I had seen and heard in Bangalore in two weeks of filming. The global competitive playing field was being leveled. The world was being flattened.

As I came to this realization, I was filled with both excitement and dread. The journalist in me was excited at having found a framework to better understand the morning headlines and to explain what was happening in the world today. Clearly Nandan was right: It is now

[26] culmination: climax
[27] essentially: basically
[28] to scribble down: to write down quickly
[29] underlying: basic

possible for more people than ever to collaborate and compete in real time with more other people on more different kinds of work from more different corners of the planet and on a more equal footing[30] than at any previous time in the history of the world – using computers, e-mail, fiber-optic networks, teleconferencing, and dynamic new software. That was what I discovered on my journey to India and beyond. And that is what this book is about. When you start to think of the world as flat, or at least in the process of flattening, a lot of things make sense in ways they did not before. But I was also excited personally, because what the flattening of the world means is that we are now connecting all the knowledge centers on the planet together into a single global network, which – if politics and terrorism do not get in the way – could usher in[31] an amazing era of prosperity, innovation, and collaboration, by companies, communities, and individuals. But contemplating the flat world also left me filled with dread,[32] professional and personal. My personal dread derived[33] from the too obvious fact that it's not only the software writers and computer geeks[34] who get empowered to collaborate on work in a flat world. It's also al-Qaeda and other terrorist networks. The playing field is not being leveled only in ways that draw in and superempower a whole new group of innovators. It's being leveled in a way that draws in and superempowers a whole new group of angry, frustrated, and humiliated men and women.

Professionally, the recognition[35] that the world was flat was unnerving[36] because I realized that this flattening had been taking place while I was sleeping, and I had missed it. I wasn't really sleeping, but I was otherwise engaged. Before 9/11,[37] I was focused on tracking globalization and exploring the tension between the "Lexus" forces of economic integration and the "Olive Tree" forces of identity and nationalism – hence[38] my 1999 book, *The Lexus and the Olive Tree.* But after 9/11, the olive tree wars became all-consuming for me. I spent almost all my time traveling in the Arab and Muslim worlds. During those years I lost the trail of globalization.

---

[30] footing: basis

[31] to usher in: to cause s.th. new to happen

[32] dread [dred]: extreme fear

[33] to derive: to come from

[34] geek: a person extremely interested in a particular thing and has no other interests

[35] recognition: understanding

[36] to unnerve: to make nervous or uncomfortable

[37] 9/11: date of the terrorist attack on the World Trade Center in New York, on September 11, 2001

[38] hence: therefore

I found that trail again on my journey to Bangalore in February 2004. Once I did, I realized that something really important had happened while I was fixated on the olive groves[39] of Kabul and Baghdad. Globalization had gone to a whole new level. If you put *The Lexus and the Olive Tree* and this book together, the broad historical argument you end up with is that there have been three great eras of globalization. The first lasted from 1492 – when Columbus set sail, opening trade between the Old World and the New World – until around 1800. I would call this era Globalization 1.0. It shrank the world from a size large to a size medium. Globalization 1.0 was about countries and muscles. That is, in Globalization 1.0, the key agent of change, the dynamic force driving the process of global integration, was how much brawn[40] – how much muscle, how much horsepower, wind power, or, later, steam power – your country had and how creatively you could deploy[41] it. In this era, countries and governments (often inspired by religion or imperialism or a combination of both) led the way in breaking down walls and knitting[42] the world together, driving global integration. In Globalization 1.0, the primary questions were: Where does my country fit into global competition and opportunities? How can I go global and collaborate with others through my country?

The second great era, Globalization 2.0, lasted roughly[43] from 1800 to 2000, interrupted by the Great Depression and World Wars I and II. This era shrank the world from a size medium to a size small. In Globalization 2.0, the key agent of change, the dynamic force driving global integration, was multinational companies. These multinationals went global for markets and labor, spearheaded[44] first by the expansion of the Dutch and English joint-stock companies[45] and the Industrial Revolution. In the first half of this era, global integration was powered by falling transportation costs, thanks to the steam engine and the railroad, and in the second half by falling telecommunication costs – thanks to the diffusion of the telegraph, telephones, the PC, satellites, fiber-optic cable, and the early version of the World Wide Web. It was during

---

[39] grove: small area of land with fruit trees
[40] brawn: muscle
[41] to deploy: to use
[42] to knit: to connect
[43] roughly ['rʌfli]: circa (*etwa*)
[44] to spearhead: to lead
[45] joint-stock company: a company that is owned by all the people who have shares (*Aktien*) in it

this era that we really saw the birth and maturation[46] of a global economy, in the sense that there was enough movement of goods and information from continent to continent for there to be a global market, with global arbitrage[47] in products and labor. The dynamic forces behind this era of globalization were breakthroughs in hardware – from steamships and railroads in the beginning to telephones and mainframe computers toward the end. And the big questions in this era were: Where does my company fit into the global economy? How does it take advantage of the opportunities? How can I go global and collaborate with others through my company? *The Lexus and the Olive Tree* was primarily about the climax of this era, an era when the walls started falling all around the world, and integration – and the backlash[48] to it – went to a whole new level. But even as the walls fell, there were still a lot of barriers to seamless[49] global integration. Remember, when Bill Clinton was elected president in 1992, virtually no one outside of government and the academy had e-mail, and when I was writing *The Lexus and the Olive Tree* in 1998, the Internet and e-commerce were just taking off.

Well, they took off – along with a lot of other things that came together while I was sleeping. And that is why I argue in this book that right around the year 2000 we entered a whole new era: Globalization 3.0. Globalization 3.0 is shrinking the world from a size small to a size tiny and flattening the playing field at the same time. And while the dynamic force in Globalization 1.0 was countries globalizing and the dynamic force in Globalization 2.0 was companies globalizing, the dynamic force in Globalization 3.0 – the force that gives it its unique character – is the newfound power for *individuals* to collaborate and compete globally. And the phenomenon that is enabling, empowering, and enjoining[50] individuals and small groups to go global so easily and so seamlessly is what I call the *flat-world platform,* which I describe in detail in this book. Just a hint:[51] The flat-world platform is the product of a convergence of the personal computer (which allowed every individual suddenly to become the author of his or her own content in digital form) with fiber-optic cable (which suddenly allowed all those individuals to access more and more digital content around the world for next to nothing) with the rise

[46] maturation: full development
[47] arbitrage: (here): the simultaneous buying and selling of goods and services
[48] backlash: a reaction in the opposite direction
[49] seamless: uninterrupted
[50] to enjoin: (here): to encourage
[51] hint: a clue

of work flow software (which enabled individuals all over the world to collaborate on that same digital content from anywhere, regardless of the distances between them). No one anticipated this convergence.[52] It just happened – right around the year 2000. And when it did, people all over the world started waking up and realizing that they had more power than ever to go global as *individuals*, they needed more than ever to think of themselves as individuals competing against other individuals all over the planet, and they had more opportunities to work with those other individuals, not just compete with them. As a result, every person now must, and can ask: Where do *I* as an individual fit into the global competition and opportunities of the day, and how can *I*, on my own, collaborate with others globally?

But Globalization 3.0 differs from the previous eras not only in how it is shrinking and flattening the world and in how it is empowering individuals. It also is different in that Globalization 1.0 and 2.0 were driven primarily by European and American individuals and businesses. Even though China actually had the biggest economy in the world in the eighteenth century, it was Western countries, companies, and explorers who were doing most of the globalizing and shaping of the system. But going forward, this will be less and less true. Because it is flattening and shrinking the world, Globalization 3.0 is going to be more and more driven not only by individuals but also by a much more diverse – non-Western, non-white – group of individuals. Individuals from every corner of the flat world are being empowered. Globalization 3.0 makes it possible for so many more people to plug in and play, and you are going to see every color of the human rainbow take part.

[...]

Flatburgers and fries

I kept moving – all the way back to my home in Bethesda, Maryland. By the time I settled back into my house from this journey to the edges of the earth, my head was spinning. But no sooner was I home than more signs of the flattening came knocking at my door. Some came in the form of headlines that would unnerve any parent concerned about where his college-age children are going to fit in. For instance,[53] Forrester Research,

[52] convergence: coming together
[53] for instance: for example

Inc., was projecting that more than three million service and professional jobs would move out of the country by 2015. But my jaw really dropped[54] when I read a July 19, 2004, article from the *International Herald Tribune* headlined: "Want Fries With Outsourcing?"

Pull off U.S. Interstate Highway 55 near Cape Girardeau, Missouri, and into the drive-through lane of a McDonald's next to the highway and you'll get fast, friendly service, even though the person taking your order is not in the restaurant – or even in Missouri. The order taker is in a call center in Colorado Springs, more than 900 miles, or 1,450 kilometers, away, connected to the customer and to the workers preparing the food by high-speed data lines. Even some restaurant jobs, it seems, are not immune to outsourcing.

The man who owns the Cape Girardeau restaurant, Shannon Davis, has linked it and three other of his 12 McDonald's franchises to the Colorado call center, which is run by another McDonald's franchisee,[55] Steven Bigari. And he did it for the same reasons that other business owners have embraced[56] call centers: lower costs, greater speed and fewer mistakes.

Cheap, quick and reliable telecommunications lines let the order takers in Colorado Springs converse with customers in Missouri, take an electronic snapshot[57] of them, display their order on a screen to make sure it is right, then forward the order and the photo to the restaurant kitchen. The photo is destroyed as soon as the order is completed, Bigari said. People picking up their burgers never know that their order traverses[58] two states and bounces back before they can even start driving to the pickup window.

Davis said that he had dreamed of doing something like this for more than a decade. "We could not wait to go with it," he added. Bigari, who created the call center for his own restaurants, was happy to oblige – for a small fee per transaction.[59]

---

[54] my jaw ... dropped: I was really surprised ...

[55] franchisee: a person or company given official permission to sell a product or service by another firm

[56] to embrace: to accept with enthusiasm

[57] snapshot: a quick picture

[58] to traverse: to travel

[59] transaction: order

The article went on to note that McDonald's Corp. said it found the call center idea interesting enough to start a test with three stores near its headquarters in Oak Brook, Illinois, with different software from that used by Bigari. "Jim Sappington, a McDonald's vice president for information technology, said that it was 'way, way too early' to tell if the call center idea would work across the thirteen thousand McDonald's restaurants in the United States ... Still, franchisees of two other McDonald's restaurants, beyond Davis's, have outsourced their drive-through ordering to Bigari in Colorado Springs. (The other restaurants are in Brainerd, Minnesota, and Norwood, Massachusetts.) Central to the system's success, Bigari said, is the way it pairs customers' photos with their orders; by increasing accuracy, the system cuts down on the number of complaints and therefore makes the service faster. In the fast-food business, time is truly money: shaving[60] even five seconds off the processing time of an order is significant,"[61] the article noted. "Bigari said he had cut order time in his dual-lane[62] drive-throughs by slightly more than 30 seconds, to about 1 minute, 5 seconds, on average. That's less than half the average of 2 minutes, 36 seconds, for all McDonald's, and among the fastest of any franchise[63] in the country, according to QSRweb.com, which tracks such things. His drive-throughs now handle 260 cars an hour, Bigari said, 30 more than they did before he started the call center ... Though his operators earn, on average, 40 cents an hour more than his line employees, he has cut his overall labor costs by a percentage point, even as drive-through sales have increased ... Tests conducted by outside companies found that Bigari's drive-throughs now make mistakes on fewer than 2 percent of all orders, down from about 4 percent before he started using the call centers, Bigari said."

Bigari "is so enthusiastic about the call center idea," the article noted, "that he has expanded it beyond the drive-through window at his seven restaurants that use the system. While he still offers counter service at those restaurants, most customers now order through the call center, using phones with credit card readers on tables in the seating area."

And I kept going east, right to my living room, where one day Ann, my wife, who is a first-grade reading teacher, pointed out to me an article about how American kids and parents are now turning to Indians for

---

[60] to shave: to cut
[61] significant: important
[62] dual lane: two different lines
[63] franchise: official permission given by a company to another company or person to sell its products or services

online tutoring. An October 2005 Associated Press report from Cochin, India, tells the whole story:

A few stars are still twinkling in the inky pre-dawn sky when Koyampurath Namitha arrives for work in a quiet suburb of this south Indian city. It's barely[64] 4:30 a.m. when she grabs a cup of coffee and joins more than two dozen colleagues, each settling into a cubicle with a computer and earphones. More than 7,000 miles away, in Glenview, Ill., outside Chicago, it's the evening of the previous day and 14-year-old Princeton John sits at his computer, barefoot and ready for his hour-long geometry lesson. The high school freshman puts on a headset with a microphone and clicks on computer software that will link him through the Internet to his tutor, Namitha, many time zones away.

It's called e-tutoring-yet another example of how modern communications, and an abundance of[65] educated, low-wage Asians, are broadening the boundaries of outsourcing and working their way into the minutiae[66] of American life, from replacing your lost credit card through reading your CAT scan[67] to helping you revive[68] your crashed computer. Princeton is one of thousands of U.S. high school students turning to tutors in India.

"Hello Princeton, how are you? How was your test?" Namitha asks. "Hello, yeah ... I'm good," Princeton replies. "It was good."

Namitha works for a company called Growing Stars, based in Cochin and Fremont, California. Princeton and his 12-year-old sister Priscilla each meet with their online math teacher twice a week. The chitchat ends quickly and a geometry worksheet pops up on Princeton's computer screen. Teacher and pupil speak to one another, type messages and use digital "pencils" to work on problems, highlight graphs and erase mistakes. Princeton scrawls[69] on something that looks like a hyped-up[70] mouse pad and it shows up on Namitha's screen. He can also use a scanner to send copies of assignments or textbook pages that he needs help understanding. "Here we go," Princeton says, as they

[64] barely: little more than
[65] abundance of: many
[66] minutiae [maɪˈnjuːʃiiː] (plural): very small details
[67] CAT scan: Computed Axial Tomography generated pictures
[68] to revive: to bring back to life
[69] to scrawl: to write
[70] to hype [haɪp]: to exaggerate

> begin a lesson on such concepts as parallel lines and complementary angles in the quiet coziness[71] of the family's suburban home ...
>
> The first e-tutoring businesses started less than three years ago, and already thousands of Indian teachers coach U.S. students in math, science or English for about $15 to $20 an hour, a fraction of the $40 to $100 that private tutoring costs in the United States ... Princeton's mother, Bessy Piusten, is pleased[72] with the results, saying her children have been getting all A's and B's since they started online tutoring about two years ago ... At the end of the session, Namitha assigns Princeton problems for their next meeting. "Homework! C'mon!" Princeton protests. "Fine, fine. But without homework, life would be wonderful," he says.

Though I was already home, I kept on moving east – to downtown Washington, D.C., right next to my office. One afternoon in the fall of 2005 I walked over to interview the U.S. trade representative, Ambassador Rob Portman, whose aide, Amy M. Wilkinson, a White House fellow,[73] told me the most unusual flat-world story. The United States and Oman had just completed negotiations on a free-trade agreement to eliminate tariffs and trade barriers between the two nations. What was unusual, though, was that Portman sealed the deal[74] via a videoconference with Maqbool Bin Ali Sultan, Oman's minister of commerce and industry, who participated virtually[75] from Muscat, the country's capital.

What could be flatter, I asked myself, than a free-trade agreement sealed using flat-screen TVs? Ms. Wilkinson later filled me in: "There were approximately 30 press folks in our conference room with notebooks in hand. Ambassador Portman stood at a podium in the front of the room. His image was projected on a digital videoconference dual screen. [The] Omani minister of commerce and industry and a roundtable of Omani press were projected on the other half of the screen. Ambassador Portman gave remarks. The Omani minister gave remarks. The session was then opened for questions. The U.S. press peppered Portman with questions. We broke and asked if the Omanis had questions. They asked questions of their minister. Then the crossover began when a U.S. reporter asked both Ambassador Portman and Minister Maqbool Bin Ali Sultan a question together. The exchange continued with U.S. press ask-

---

71 coziness: comfort
72 pleased: happy
73 fellow: (here): ~~young university graduate appointed for a limited time to gain experience~~
74 to seal the deal: to close the deal
75 virtually: (here): via the internet rather than being physically present

ing the Omani minister questions and vice versa. The meeting ended with Portman [on one side of the screen] extending his hand in a 'virtual handshake.' The Omani minister [on the other] did the same. It looked a bit funny and got a few chuckles but seemed to work for everyone. The process included more people than if teams had traveled in either direction. Connecting digitally eliminated a tremendous amount of wear and tear and seemed to satisfy everyone around the 'virtual table.' "

I recalled that virtual deal signing one day months later when I telephoned my stockbroker, Mark Madden at UBS,[76] and he put me on hold. While I was waiting, a commercial for UBS played over and over. It noted that global markets today were more accessible and interconnected than ever before – and that, because of this change, UBS services were now available in "only" two locations: "Everywhere, and right next to you."

As UBS explained in the commercial: "Because financial solutions have no borders or boundaries, UBS puts investment analysts in markets across the globe. We have specialists worldwide in wealth management, asset[77] management, and investment banking. So your UBS financial adviser can draw on a network of resources to provide you with an appropriate solution – and shrink the world to a manageable size."

I loved that concept of a company with only two offices – "everywhere, and right next to you" – because it captured perfectly the way the flattening of the world allows companies to be more global than ever and, yet, at the same time, more personal than ever.

Some of the signs of flattening back home, though, had nothing to do with economics. A month before the 2004 election I had appeared on the CBS News Sunday morning show *Face the Nation,* hosted by veteran correspondent Bob Schieffer. CBS had been in the news a lot in previous weeks because of Dan Rather's *60 Minutes* report about President George W. Bush's Air National Guard service that turned out to be based on bogus[78] documents. After the show that Sunday, Schieffer mentioned that the oddest thing had happened to him the week before. When he walked out of the CBS studio, a young reporter was waiting for him on the sidewalk. This isn't all that unusual, because as with all the Sunday-morning shows, the major networks – CBS, NBC, ABC, CNN, and Fox – always send crews to one another's studios to grab exit interviews with the guests. But this young man, Schieffer explained, was not from a major network. He politely introduced himself as a re-

---

[76] UBS: a Swiss investment firm and bank

[77] asset: anything of value, such as property or equipment

[78] bogus ['bəʊgəs]: falsified

porter for a Web site called InDC Journal and asked whether he could ask Schieffer a few questions. Schieffer, being a polite fellow, said sure. The young man interviewed him on a device Schieffer did not recognize and then asked if he could take his picture. A picture? Schieffer noticed that the young man had no camera. He didn't need one. He turned his cell phone[79] around and snapped Schieffer's picture.

"So I came in the next morning and looked up this Web site and there was my picture and the interview and there were already three hundred comments about it," said Schieffer, who, though keenly[80] aware of online journalism, was nevertheless taken aback[81] at the incredibly fast, low-cost, and solo manner in which this young man had put him up in lights.

I was intrigued by this story, so I tracked down the young man from InDC Journal. His name is Bill Ardolino, and he is a very thoughtful guy. I conducted my own interview with him online – how else? –and began by asking about what equipment he was using as a one-man network/newspaper.

"I used a minuscule MP3 player/digital recorder (three and a half inches by two inches) to get the recording, and a separate small digital camera phone to snap his picture," said Ardolino. "Not quite as sexy as an all-in-one phone/camera/recorder (which does exist), but a statement on the ubiquity[82] and miniaturization of technology nonetheless. I carry this equipment around D.C. at all times because, hey, you never know. What's perhaps more startling is how well Mr. Schieffer thought on his feet, after being jumped on by some stranger with interview questions. He blew me away." [83]

Ardolino said the MP3 player cost him about $125. It is "primarily designed to play music," he explained, but it also "comes prepackaged as a digital recorder that creates a WAV sound file that can be uploaded back to a computer ... Basically, I'd say that the barrier to entry to do journalism that requires portable, ad hoc[84] recording equipment, is [now] about $100–$200 to $300 if you add a camera, $400 to $500 for a pretty nice recorder and a pretty nice camera. [But] $200 is all that you need to get the job done."

What prompted[85] him to become his own news network?

---

[79] cell phone: mobile phone
[80] to be keenly aware of: to be well informed about s.th.
[81] to be taken aback: to be surprised
[82] ubiquity: omnipresence
[83] to blow away (colloquial): to really impress someone
[84] ad hoc (Latin): not planned in advance
[85] to prompt: to cause

"Being an independent journalist is a hobby that sprang from my frustration about biased,[86] incomplete, selective, and/or incompetent information gathering by the mainstream[87] media," explained Ardolino, who describes himself as a "center-right libertarian." "Independent journalism and its relative, blogging, are expressions of market forces – a need is not being met by current information sources. I started taking pictures and doing interviews of the antiwar rallies in D.C., because the media was grossly misrepresenting the nature of the groups that were organizing the gatherings – unrepentant[88] Marxists, explicit and implicit supporters of terror, etc. I originally chose to use humor as a device, but I've since branched out.[89] Do I have more power, power to get my message out, yes. The Schieffer interview actually brought in about twenty-five thousand visits in twenty-four hours. My peak[90] day since I've started was fifty-five thousand when I helped break 'Rathergate'[91] ... I interviewed the first forensics expert[92] in the Dan Rather National Guard story, and he was then specifically picked up by *The Washington Post, Chicago Sun-Times, Globe,* NYT, etc., within forty-eight hours.

"The pace of information gathering and correction in the CBS fake memo story was astounding," he continued. "It wasn't just that CBS News 'stonewalled'[93] after the fact, it was arguably that they couldn't keep up with an army of dedicated[94] fact-checkers. The speed and openness of the medium is something that runs rings around[95] the old process ... I'm a twenty-nine-year-old marketing manager [who] always wanted to write for a living but hated the AP[96] style book. As überblogger[97] Glenn Reynolds likes to say, blogs have given the people a chance to stop yelling at their TV and have a say in the process. I think that they serve as sort of a 'fifth estate' that works in conjunction with the mainstream

[86] biased: partisan or not objective
[87] mainstream: dominant
[88] unrepentant: showing no shame about your beliefs or actions
[89] to branch out: to diversify
[90] peak [pi:k]: with the greatest amount
[91] Rathergate: a play on the "Watergate" scandal which led to President Nixon's resignation
[92] forensics expert: a scientist or doctor who helps in the investigation of a crime
[93] to stonewall (colloquial): to be uncooperative and obstructive
[94] staunch: dedicated
[95] to run rings around (colloquial): to be much better than
[96] AP: Associated Press, a news agency
[97] überblogger (slang): an example of how the German prefix "über" is now used in English to mean "super"

media (often by keeping an eye on them or feeding them raw info) and potentially function as a journalism and commentary farm system[98] that provides a new means to establish success.

"Like many facets of the topic that you're talking about in your book, there are good and bad aspects of the development. The splintering of media makes for a lot of incoherence[99] or selective cognition (look at our country's polarization), but it also decentralizes power and provides a better guarantee that the *complete* truth *is* out there ... somewhere ... in pieces."

On any given day one can come across stories like that one – stories that tell you that old hierarchies are being flattened, that the playing field is being leveled, and that people who understand this transformation can wield[100] more power than ever. I was shuffling through[101] the June 25, 2005, edition of the *Financial Times* when a headline caught my eye: "Google Lures[102] More Talent." The article seemed straightforward enough, detailing how Google had managed to hire[103] legendary technologist Louis Monier away from eBay, where he was heading advanced technology. But I was brought up short[104] by a paragraph in the middle of the article: "Mr. Monier revealed his motives [for leaving eBay] in an e-mail exchange with blogger John Battelle, who spread the news on his website, battellemedia.com." In other words, a top blogger whose expertise is Google broke the story, and the giant *Financial Times* had to quote his one-man Web site to be on top of the story itself.

Micah L. Sifry, an expert on the interplay of politics and technology, summarized[105] the phenomenon well in an essay in *The Nation* (November 22, 2004): "The era of top-down politics – where campaigns, institutions and journalism were cloistered[106] communities powered by hard-to-amass capital – is over. Something wilder, more engaging and infinitely[107] more satisfying to individual participants is arising alongside the old order."

I offer the Schieffer-Ardolino and *Financial Times* cases as just two examples of how the flattening of the world has happened faster and

---

[98] farm system: part of an organization which trains promising new talent
[99] incoherence: lack of clarity
[100] to wield [wiːld]: to make use of
[101] to shuffle through: (here): to scan the headlines
[102] to lure: (here): to attract
[103] to hire: to employ
[104] to be brought up short: to be surprised
[105] to summarize: to present in a short form
[106] to be cloistered: to be protected from outside interference
[107] infinitely: endlessly

changed rules, roles, and relationships more quickly than social science can capture. And, though I know it is a cliché, I have to say it nevertheless: *You ain't seen nothing' yet.*[108] As I detail in the next chapter, we are entering a phase where we are going to see the digitization, virtualization, and automation of more and more everything. The gains in productivity will be staggering[109] for those countries, companies, and individuals who can absorb[110] the new technological tools. And we are entering a phase where more people than ever before in the history of the world are going to have access to these tools – as innovators, as collaborators, and, alas,[111] even as terrorists. You say you want a revolution? Well, the real information revolution is about to begin. I call this new phase Globalization 3.0 because it followed Globalization 2.0, but I think this new era of globalization will prove to be such a difference of degree that it will be seen, in time, as a difference in kind. That is why I introduced the idea that the world has gone from round to flat. Everywhere you turn, hierarchies are being challenged from below or are transforming themselves from top-down structures into more horizontal and collaborative ones.

"'Globalization' is the word we came up with to describe the changing relationships between governments and big businesses," said David Rothkopf, a former senior Department of Commerce official in the Clinton administration and now a private strategic consultant. "But what is going on today is a much broader, much more profound phenomenon." It is not simply about how governments, business, and people communicate, not just about how organizations interact, but is about the emergence[112] of completely new social, political, and business models. "It is about things that impact[113] some of the deepest, most ingrained[114] aspects of society right down to the nature of the social contract,"[115] added Rothkopf. "What happens if the political entity in which you are located no longer corresponds to a job that takes place in cyberspace, or no longer really encompasses[116] workers collaborating with other workers in different corners of the globe, or no longer really captures

---

[108] you ain't seen nothing yet (slang): title of a song by Bachman Turner Overdrive meaning it's only just begun
[109] staggering (fig.): so amazing that it causes you to lose your balance
[110] to absorb: to integrate
[111] alas: expression used to express concern
[112] emergence: appearance
[113] to impact: to influence
[114] ingrained: firmly established
[115] social contract: agreement between the government and the governed
[116] to encompass: to include

products produced in multiple places simultaneously? Who regulates the work? Who taxes it? Who should benefit from those taxes?"

I am convinced that the flattening of the world, if it continues, will be seen in time as one of those fundamental shifts or inflection[117] points, like Gutenberg's invention of the printing press, the rise of the nation-state, or the Industrial Revolution – each of which, in its day, noted Rothkopf, produced changes in the role of individuals, the role and form of governments, the ways business was done and wars were fought, the role of women, the forms religion and art took, and the way science and research were conducted, not to mention the political labels that we as a civilization have assigned to ourselves and to our enemies. "There are certain pivot points[118] or watersheds[119] in history that are greater than others because the changes they produced were so sweeping, multifaceted, and hard to predict[120] at the time," Rothkopf said.

If the prospect[121] of this flattening – and all of the pressures, dislocations, and opportunities accompanying it – makes you uneasy about the future, you are neither wrong nor alone. Whenever civilization has gone through a major technological revolution, the world has changed in profound and unsettling[122] ways. But there is something about the flattening of the world that is going to be qualitatively different from the great changes of previous eras: the speed and breadth[123] with which it is taking hold. The introduction of printing happened over a period of decades and for a long time affected only a relatively small part of the planet. Same with the Industrial Revolution. This flattening process is happening at warp speed[124] and directly or indirectly touching a lot more people on the planet at once. The faster and broader this transition to a new era, the greater the potential for disruption,[125] as opposed to an orderly transfer of power from the old winners to the new winners.

To put it another way, the experiences of the high-tech companies in the last few decades that failed to navigate the rapid changes brought about in their marketplace by these types of forces may be a warning to all the businesses, institutions, and nation-states that are now facing

---

[117] inflection: (here): having to do with a great change
[118] pivot point: *Dreh- und Angelpunkt*
[119] watershed: (here): an important event that serves as a dividing line
[120] to predict: to say how things will be
[121] prospect: possibility
[122] to unsettle: to disturb
[123] breadth: the degree to which
[124] warp speed (slang): a term from science fiction meaning the fastest possible speed
[125] disruption: an unwanted break

these inevitable, even predictable, changes but lack the leadership, flexibility, and imagination to adapt – not because they are not smart or aware, but because the speed of change is simply overwhelming[126] them.

And that is why the great challenge for our time will be to absorb these changes in ways that do not overwhelm people or leave them behind. None of this will be easy. But this is our task. It is inevitable and unavoidable. It is the ambition of this book to offer a framework for how to think about this task and manage it to our maximum benefit.

I have shared with you in this chapter how I personally discovered that the world is flat. The next chapter details how it got that way.

Info Box

Friedman's 10 Flatteners

Flattener # 1: 11/9/89

This is the actual date of the fall of the Berlin wall and the symbolic date of the collapse of the Communist worldview. The sudden disappearance of this physical barrier transformed the world by creating an open and ideologically uniformed international system.

Flattener # 2: 8/9/95

This is the date that the Netscape browser company became a stock company. It was the invention of such browser technology that made the World Wide Web (WWW) the powerful tool it has become.

Flattener # 3: Work Flow Software

Having a common language by which different computers could communicate allowed complex tasks to be split up and worked on at various sites around the world.

126 to overwhelm: to overrun (*überwältigen*)

Flattener # 4: Uploading

By being able to "publish" media content directly on the web, people around the world became directly involved in the dissemination of information.

Flattener # 5: Outsourcing

Although this term has taken on negative connotations, it merely refers to giving work which was being done internally to an external company which has more expertise in the field, or can do it cheaper.

Flattener # 6: Offshoring

Different from outsourcing, this is where a company actually moves a whole department to another country for reasons such as lower wages, a more educated workforce, lower taxes, or better infrastructure.

Flattener # 7: Supply-Chaining

The orchestration of numerous stages in production and delivery processes which helps to guide goods from the manufacturers to the stores.

Flattener # 8: Insourcing

This involves integrating part of another company into your own to provide a service for you.

Flattener # 9: In-forming

This represents the ability people now have to select the information and entertainment they want, when they want it.

Flattener # 10: The Steroids

Like the doping chemicals which increase an athlete's performance, the increasing mobility of electronic devises intensifies the effects of the other nine flatteners. Friedman also says that their impact is added to by what he calls the "triple convergence." These are the ability to combine new technologies in creative ways, the high amount of international cooperation, and the increased amount of competition from places that were previously outside the global economy.

Chapter 2: The Ten Forces That Flattened the World

Flattener # 1: 11/9/89

The New Age of Creativity: When the Walls Came Down and the Windows Went Up

The first time I saw the Berlin Wall, it already had a hole in it.

It was December 1990, and I was traveling to Berlin with the reporters covering secretary of state James A. Baker III. The Berlin Wall had been breached[127] a year earlier, on November 9, 1989. Yes, in a wonderful kabalistic[128] accident of dates, the Berlin Wall fell on 11/9. The wall, even in its punctured and broken state, was still an ugly scar across Berlin. Secretary Baker was making his first visit to see this crumbled monument to Soviet communism. I was standing next to him with a small group of reporters. "It was a foggy, overcast day," Baker recalled in his memoir, *The Politics of Diplomacy,* "and in my raincoat, I felt like a character in a John le Carré[129] novel. But as I peered through a crack in the Wall [near the Reichstag] and saw the high-resolution[130] drabness[131] that characterizes East Berlin, I realized that the ordinary men and women of East Germany, peacefully and persistently, had taken matters into their own hands. This was their revolution." After Baker finished looking through the wall and moved along, we reporters took turns peering through the same jagged[132] concrete hole. I brought a couple of chunks of the wall home for my daughters. I remember thinking how unnatural it looked – indeed, what a bizarre thing it was, this cement wall snaking across[133] a modern city for the sole purpose of preventing the people on the other side from enjoying, even glimpsing,[134] freedom.

---

[127] to breach: to break a hole in a wall

[128] kabalistic: reference to a sect of the Jewish religion which claims to find esoteric meaning in coded relationships

[129] John le Carré (actual name, Daniel Cornwell, 1931–): English writer specializing in spy novels

[130] high-resolution: (here): easily seen, obvious

[131] drabness: the quality of being dull and colorless

[132] jagged: irregular with sharp edges

[133] to snake across: to not move in a straight line

[134] to glimpse: to see for a second or two

The fall of the Berlin Wall on 11/9/89 unleashed[135] forces that ultimately liberated all the captive peoples of the Soviet Empire. But it actually did so much more. It tipped the balance of power across the world toward those advocating democratic, consensual, free-market-oriented governance, and away from those advocating authoritarian rule with centrally planned economies. The Cold War had been a struggle between two economic systems – capitalism and communism – and with the fall of the wall, there was only one system left and everyone had to orient himself or herself to it one way or another. Henceforth, more and more economies would be governed from the ground up, by the interests, demands, and aspirations[136] of the people, rather than from the top down, by the interests of some narrow ruling clique. Within two years, there was no Soviet Empire to hide behind anymore or to prop up autocratic regimes in Asia, the Middle East, Africa, or Latin America. If you were not a democracy or a democratizing society, if you continued to hold fast to highly regulated or centrally planned economics, you were seen as being on the wrong side of history.

For some, particularly among the older generations, this was an unwelcome transformation. Communism was a great system for making people equally poor. In fact, there was no better system in the world for that than communism. Capitalism made people unequally rich, and for some who were used to the plodding,[137] limited, but secure Socialist lifestyle – where a job, a house, an education, and a pension were all guaranteed, even if they were meager[138] – the fall of the Berlin Wall was deeply unsettling. But for many others, it was a get-out-of-jail-free card.[139] That is why the fall of the Berlin Wall was felt in so many more places than just Berlin, and why its fall was such a world-flattening event.

Indeed, to appreciate[140] the far-reaching flattening effects of the fall of the Berlin Wall, it's always best to talk to non-Germans or non-Russians. Tarun Das was heading the Confederation of Indian Industry when the wall fell in Berlin, and he saw its ripple effect[141] felt all the way to India. "We had this huge mass of regulation and controls and bureaucracy," he

[135] to unleash: to release
[136] aspiration: desire
[137] plodding: monotonous
[138] meager: lacking in quantity or quality
[139] get out of jail free card (colloquial): a card from the game "Monopoly" which allows you to gain your freedom
[140] to appreciate: to understand the significance of something
[141] ripple effect: like the expanding waves created on the surface of calm water caused by a stone falling into it

recalled. "Nehru had come to power [after the end of British colonial rule] and had a huge country to manage, and no experience of running a country. The U.S. was busy with Europe and Japan and the Marshall Plan. So Nehru looked north, across the Himalayas, and sent his team of economists to Moscow. They came back and said that this country [the Soviet Union] was amazing. They allocate[142] resources, they give licenses, there is a planning commission that decides everything, and the country moves. So we took that model and forgot that we had a private sector ... That private sector got put under this wall of regulation. By 1991, the private sector was there, but under wraps,[143] and there was mistrust about business. They made profits! The entire infrastructure from 1947 to 1991 was government-owned ... [The burden of state ownership] almost bankrupted the country. We were not able to pay our debts[144] ... Sure, we might have won a couple of wars with Pakistan, but that did not give the nation confidence."

In 1991, with India running out of hard currency, Manmohan Singh, the finance minister at that time (and now the prime minister), decided that India had to open its economy. "Our Berlin Wall fell," said Das, "and it was like unleashing[145] a caged tiger. Trade controls were abolished. We were always at 3 percent growth, the so-called Hindu rate of growth – slow, cautious, and conservative. To make [better returns], you had to go to America. Well, three years later [after the 1991 reforms] we were at 7 percent rate of growth. To hell with poverty! Now to make it you could stay in India and become one of *Forbes's*[146] richest people in the world ... All the years of socialism and controls had taken us downhill to the point where we had only $ 1 billion in foreign currency. Today we have $118 billion ... We went from quiet self-confidence to outrageous ambition in a decade."

The fall of the Berlin Wall didn't just help flatten the alternatives to free-market capitalism and unlock enormous pent-up[147] energies for hundreds of millions of people in places like India, Brazil, China, and the former Soviet Empire. It also allowed us to think about the world differently – to see it as more of a seamless whole. Because the Berlin Wall was not only blocking our way; it was blocking our sight – our

142 to allocate: to distribute
143 under wraps: kept hidden or secret
144 debt [det]: the money you owe
145 to unleash (fig.): to to set free
146 Forbes: one of the major American business magazines well-known for its lists of the richest people in America and the world
147 pent-up: repressed

ability to think about the world as a single market, a single ecosystem, and a single community. Before 1989, you could have an Eastern policy or a Western policy, but it was hard to think about having a "global" policy. Amartya Sen, the Nobel Prize-winning Indian economist now teaching at Harvard, once remarked to me that "the Berlin Wall was not only a symbol of keeping people inside East Germany – it was a way of preventing a kind of global view of our future. We could not think globally about the world when the Berlin Wall was there. We could not think about the world as a whole." There is a lovely story in Sanskrit, Sen added, about a frog that is born in a well[148] and stays in the well and lives its entire life in the well. "It has a worldview that consists of the well," he said. "That was what the world was like for many people on the planet before the fall of the wall. When it fell, it was like the frog in the well was suddenly able to communicate with frogs in all the other wells ... If I celebrate the fall of the wall, it is because I am convinced of how much we can learn from each other. Most knowledge is learning from the other across the border."

Yes, the world became a better place to live in after 11/9, because each outbreak of freedom stimulated another outbreak, and that process in and of itself had a flattening effect across societies, strengthening those below and weakening those above. "Women's freedom," noted Sen, citing just one example, "which promotes women's literacy,[149] tends to reduce fertility[150] and child mortality and increase the employment opportunities for women, which then affects the political dialogue and gives women the opportunity for a greater role in local self-government."

Finally, the fall of the wall did not just open the way for more people to tap into[151] one another's knowledge pools. It also paved the way[152] for the adoption of common standards – standards on how economies should be run, on how accounting should be done, on how banking should be conducted, on how PCs should be made, and on how economics papers should be written. I discuss this more later, but suffice it to say here that common standards create a flatter, more level playing field. To put it another way, the fall of the wall enhanced the free movement of best practices. When an economic or technological standard emerged and proved itself on the world stage, it was much more quickly adopted after the wall

[148] well: a hole in the ground from which water is drawn
[149] literacy: the ability to read
[150] fertility: birth rates
[151] to tap into: to access
[152] to pave the way (fig.): to make s.th. possible

was out of the way. In Europe alone, the fall of the wall opened the way for the formation of the European Union and its expansion from fifteen to twenty-five countries. That, in combination with the advent of the euro as a common currency, has created a single economic zone out of a region once divided by an Iron Curtain.

While the positive effects of the wall coming down were immediately apparent, the cause of the wall's fall was not so clear. There *was* no single cause. To some degree the termites just ate away at the foundations of the Soviet Union, which were already weakened by the system's own internal contradictions[153] and inefficiencies; to some degree the Reagan administration's military buildup in Europe forced the Kremlin to bankrupt itself paying for warheads; and to some degree Mikhail Gorbachev's futile[154] efforts to reform something that was unreformable brought communism to an end. But if I had to point to one factor as first among equals, it was the information revolution that began in the early to mid-1980s. Totalitarian systems depend on a monopoly of information and force, and too much information started to slip through the Iron Curtain, thanks to the spread of fax machines, telephones, and, eventually, the personal computer.

Following the pioneering release of the Apple II home computer by Steve Jobs and Steve Wozniak in 1977, the first IBM PC (personal computer) hit the markets in 1981. The first version of the Windows operating system launched in 1985, and the breakthrough version that made IBM PCs much more user-friendly – Windows 3.0 – shipped on May 22, 1990, only six months after the wall went down. While the fall of the wall eliminated a physical and geopolitical barrier – one that held back information, stood in the way of shared standards, and kept us from having a view of the world as a single unified community – the rise of the Windows-enabled PC, which really popularized personal computing, eliminated another hugely important barrier: the limit on the amount of information that any single individual could amass, author, manipulate, and diffuse.[155]

"The Windows-powered PC enabled millions of individuals, for the first time ever, to become authors of their own content in digital form, which meant that content could be shared far and wide," explained

---

[153] contradiction: situation in which different actions or ideas are in opposition to each other

[154] futile [ˈfjuːtaɪl]: ineffective

[155] to diffuse [dɪˈfjuːz]: to spread

Craig J. Mundie, a chief[156] technical officer for Microsoft. Over time the Apple-IBM-Windows revolution enabled the digital representation of all the important forms of expression – words, music, numeric data, maps, photographs, and eventually voice and video. It also, said Mundie, "created an army of people able to create this digital content more easily and cheaply than ever before – from their desktops, kitchens, bedrooms, and basements – instead of being required to access a big mainframe computer that was largely restricted for business purposes." Suddenly ordinary people could get the benefit of computing without being programmers.

It is impossible to exaggerate how important this was to the flattening of the world. The rise of the Windows-enabled PC, combined with the fall of the Wall, set in motion the whole flattening process. To be sure, men and women have long been authoring their own content, beginning with drawings on cave walls up through Gutenberg and the typewriter. But the Windows-enabled PCs and Apples made it possible for individuals to author their own content right from their desktops *in digital form.* And those last three words are critical. Because once people could author their own content in digital form – in the form of computer bits and bytes – they could manipulate it on computer screens in ways that made individuals so much more productive. And with the steady advances in telecommunications, they would soon be able to disseminate their own digital content in so many new ways to so many more people. Think of what one person can do with pen and paper. Think of what one person can do with a typewriter. And then think of what one person can now do with a PC.

One of Bill Gates's early mottoes for Microsoft, which he cofounded, was that the company's goal was to give every individual "IAYF" – information at your fingertips. When I said earlier that this era of Globalization 3.0 is about individuals globalizing themselves, that was largely made possible by the Apple and Windows-enabled IBM PCs and their many clones. They are the tools that gave *individuals* the power to author, shape, and disseminate information at their fingertips.

"People said, 'Wow, there is an asset[157] here, and we should take advantage of it,' " said Microsoft's Mundie. And the more established Windows became as the primary operating system, "the more programmers went out and wrote applications for rich-world businesses to put on their computers, so they could do lots of new and different business tasks, which

[156] chief: top
[157] asset: s.th. that is valuable and useful

started to enhance[158] productivity even more. Tens of millions of people around the world became programmers to make the PC do whatever they wanted in their own languages. Windows was eventually translated into thirty-eight languages [with more being added all the time]. People were able to become familiar with the PC in their own languages."

In this same time period, some people other than scientists started to discover that if they bought a PC and a dial-up modem, they could connect their PCs to their telephones and send e-mails through private Internet service providers – like CompuServe and America Online. "The diffusion of personal computers, fax machines, Windows, and dial-up modems connected to a global telephone network all came together in the late 1980s and early 1990s to create the basic platform that started the global information revolution," argued Mundie. The key was the melding of them all together into a single interoperable system. That happened, said Mundie, once we had in crude[159] form a standardized computing platform – the IBM PC–along with a standardized graphical user interface for word processing and spreadsheets[160] – Windows – along with a standardized tool for communication – dial-up modems and the global phone network. Once we had that basic interoperable platform, then the killer[161] applications – spreadsheets and word processing – drove its diffusion far and wide.

And once more and more people connected their Windows-enabled PCs with that global communications platform, which spread even more quickly after 1989, when the Berlin Wall came down (and China and India started opening to the global economy), there was nothing to stop the digital representation of everything – words, music, photos, data, video – and then the global exchange of all that digital information. The political constraint on individual reach[162] collapsed with the fall of the Berlin Wall (though of course large swaths[163] of repression still exist), and the practical constraint on individual reach collapsed with the rise of the Apple and Windows-enabled, modem-connected IBM PC. This coincidental breakthrough suddenly gave individuals in this flattening world both reach and scale–reach because they could create content in so many new and different ways and scale because they could share their content with so many more people.

---

[158] to enhance: to increase
[159] crude: unrefined
[160] spreadsheet: a sheet of paper formatted for bookkeeping as typical of *excel* ™
[161] killer (slang): extremely effective
[162] individual reach: how far individuals could go
[163] swath: area

As new and exciting as this breakthrough was compared to what existed before, it was nothing compared to what would come later. "This [initial] platform was constrained[164] by too many architectural limits," said Mundie. "There was missing infrastructure." The Internet as we know it today – with seemingly magical transmission protocols that can connect everyone and everything – had not yet emerged. Back then, networks had only very basic protocols for exchanging files and e-mail messages. Yes, AOL users could communicate with CompuServe users, but it was neither simple nor reliable. People could write new applications that allowed selected systems to work together, but in general this was limited to planned exchanges between PCs within the network of a single company. As a result, said Mundie, "a huge amount of data and creativity was accumulating in all those computers," but there was no easy, interoperable way to share it and mold it.

Nevertheless, this period from 11/9 to the mid-1990s led to a huge advance in personal empowerment. Looking back, one can say that it was the age of "Me and my machine can now talk to each other better and faster, so that I personally can do more tasks" and the age of "Me and my machine can now talk to a few friends and some other people in my company better and faster, so we can become more productive."

As I said, this level of connectivity surely helped to put the nail in the coffin[165] of communism, because the very tools that were being used to improve productivity in the West (PCs, faxes, modems), even though much scarcer in the East, vastly[166] improved horizontal person-to-person communication there, to the detriment of[167] top-down Communist systems.

Flattener # 5: outsourcing

Y2K

India has had its ups and downs since it achieved independence on August 15, 1947, but in some ways it might be remembered as the luckiest country in the history of the late twentieth century.

[164] to constrain: to limit
[165] coffin: *Sarg*
[166] vastly: greatly
[167] to the detriment of: resulting in harm to s.o. or s.th.

Until recently, India was what is known in the banking world as "the second buyer." You always want to be the second buyer in business – the person who buys the hotel or the golf course or the shopping mall after the first owner has gone bankrupt and its assets are being sold by the bank at ten cents on the dollar. Well, the first buyers of all the cable laid by all those fiber-optic cable companies – which thought they were going to get endlessly rich in an endlessly expanding digital universe – were their American shareholders. When the bubble burst, they were left holding either worthless or much diminished[168] stock. The Indians, in effect, got to be the second buyers of the fiber-optics companies.

They didn't actually purchase[169] the shares – they just benefited from the overcapacity in fiber optics, which meant that they and their American clients got to use all that cable practically for free. This was a huge stroke of luck for India (and to a lesser degree for China, the former Soviet Union, and Eastern Europe), because what is the history of modern India? While India certainly had natural resources to mine (coal, iron ore, diamonds), with so many mouths to feed, it couldn't just live off them – not even close. So instead India mined the brains of its own people, educating a relatively large slice of its elites in the sciences, engineering, and medicine. In 1951, to his enduring credit,[170] Jawaharlal Nehru, India's first prime minister, set up the first of India's seven Indian Institutes of Technology (IIT) in the eastern city of Kharagpur. In the fifty-five years since then, hundreds of thousands of Indians have competed to gain entry and then graduate from these IITs and their private-sector equivalents (as well as the six Indian Institutes of Management, which teach business administration). Given India's one-billion-plus population, this competition produces a phenomenal knowledge meritocracy. It's like a factory, churning out[171] and exporting some of the most gifted engineering, computer science, and software talent on the globe.

This, alas, was one of the few things India did right. Because its often dysfunctional political system, coupled with Nehru's preference for pro-Soviet, Socialist economics, ensured that up until the mid-1990s India could not provide good jobs for most of those talented engineers. So America got to be the second buyer of India's brainpower! If you were a smart, educated Indian, the only way you could fulfill your potential was by leaving the country and, ideally, going to America, where some

[168] to diminish: to decrease
[169] to purchase: to buy
[170] to his enduring credit: an achievement that is still worthy of praise
[171] to churn out (colloquial): to produce quickly and in great amounts

twenty-five thousand graduates of India's top engineering schools have settled since 1953, greatly enriching America's knowledge pool thanks to their education, which was subsidized[172] by Indian taxpayers.

"The IITs became islands of excellence by not allowing the general debasement[173] of the Indian system to lower their exacting standards," noted *The Wall Street Journal* (April 16, 2003). 'You couldn't bribe[174] your way to get into an IIT ... Candidates are accepted only if they pass a grueling[175] entrance exam. The government does not interfere with the curriculum, and the workload is demanding ... Arguably, it is harder to get into an IIT than into Harvard or the Massachusetts Institute of Technology ... IIT alumnus Vinod Khosla, who co-founded Sun Microsystems, said: 'When I finished IIT Delhi and went to Carnegie Mellon[176] for my Masters, I thought I was cruising[177] all the way because it was so easy relative to the education I got at IIT.'"

For most of their first fifty years, these IITs were one of the greatest bargains America ever had. It was as if someone installed a brain drain that filled up in New Delhi and emptied in Palo Alto [California]. Roughly one of four HT grads[178] ended up in the United States – so many that the American IIT expats[179] have their own organization in the United States and hold an annual convention here.

And then along came Netscape, the 1996 telecom deregulation, and Global Crossing and its fiber-optic friends. The world got flattened and that whole deal got turned on its head. "India had no resources and no infrastructure," said Dinakar Singh, one of the most respected young hedge fund managers on Wall Street, whose parents graduated from an IIT and then immigrated to America, where he was born. "It produced people with quality and by quantity. But many of them rotted[180] on the docks of India like vegetables. Only a relative few could get on ships and get out. Not anymore, because we built this ocean crosser, called fiber-optic cable ... For decades you had to leave India to be a professional ... Now you can plug into the world from India. You don't have to go to Yale and go to work for Goldman Sachs [as I did.]"

---

[172] to subsidize: to give financial support
[173] debasement: the act of making s.th. less valuable
[174] to bribe: to give someone money for a favor
[175] grueling: extremely difficult
[176] Carnegie Mellon: elite technical university in Pittsburgh, PA, USA
[177] to cruise [kru:z]: (here): to do well without much effort
[178] HT grad: high techology graduate
[179] expat: expatriate: s.o. who lives in a foreign country
[180] to rot: to go to waste

India could never have afforded to pay for the bandwidth to connect brainy India with high-tech America, so American shareholders paid for it. Sure, overinvestment can be good. The overinvestment in railroads turned out to be a great boon[181] for the American economy. "But the railroad overinvestment was confined to your own country and so too were the benefits," said Singh. In the case of the digital railroads, "it was the foreigners who benefited." India got to ride for free.

It is fun to talk to Indians who were around at precisely the moment when American companies started to discover they could draw on India's brainpower in India. One of them is Vivek Paul, now the president of Wipro, the Indian software giant. "In many ways the Indian information technology [outsourcing] revolution began with General Electric coming over. We're talking the late 1980s and early '90s. At the time, Texas Instruments was doing some chip design in India. Some of their key designers [in America] were Indians, and they basically let them go back home and work from there [using the rather crude communications networks that existed then to stay in touch].[182] At that time, I was heading up the operations for GE Medical Systems in Bangalore. [GE's chairman] Jack Welch came to India in 1989 and was completely taken by India as a source of intellectual advantage for GE. Jack would say, 'India is a developing country with a developed intellectual capability.' He saw a talent pool that could be leveraged.[183] So he said, 'We spend a lot of money doing software. Couldn't we do some work for our IT department here?' " Because India had closed its market to foreign technology companies, like IBM, Indian companies had started their own factories to make PCs and servers, and Welch felt that if they could do it for themselves, they could do it for GE.

To pursue[184] the project, Welch sent a team headed by GE's chief information officer over to India to check out the possibilities. Paul was also filling in as GE's business development manager for India at the time. "So it was my job to escort[185] the corporate CIO,[186] in early 1990, on his first trip," he recalled. "They had come with some pilot projects to get the ball rolling.[187] I remember in the middle of the night going to pick them up at the Delhi airport with a caravan of Indian cars, Ambassadors,

[181] boon: s.th. that is very helpful
[182] to stay in touch: to keep in contact
[183] to leverage: to exploit
[184] to pursue: to continue following
[185] to escort: to guide s.o. around
[186] CIO: chief investment officer
[187] to get the ball rolling (colloquial): to get started

based on a very dated 1950s Morris Minor design. Everyone in the government drove one. So we had a five-car caravan and we were driving back from the airport to town. I was in the back car, and at one point we heard this loud bang, and I thought, What happened? I shot to the front, and the lead car's hood had flown off and smashed the windshield – with these GE people inside! So this whole caravan of GE execs[188] pulls over to the side of the road, and I could just hear them saying to themselves, 'This is the place we're going to get software from?' "

Fortunately for India, the GE team was not discouraged by the poor quality of Indian cars. GE decided to sink roots,[189] starting a joint development project with Wipro. Other companies were trying different models. But this was still pre-fiber-optic days. Simon & Schuster, the book publisher, for instance, would ship its books over to India and pay Indians $50 a month (compared to $1,000 a month in the United States) to type them by hand into computers, converting the books into digitized electronic files that could be edited or amended[190] easily in the future – particularly dictionaries, which constantly need updating. In 1991, Manmohan Singh, then India's finance minister, began opening the Indian economy for foreign investment and introducing competition into the Indian telecom industry to bring down prices. To attract more foreign investment, Singh made it much easier for companies to set up satellite downlink stations in Bangalore, so they could skip over the Indian phone system and connect with their home bases in America, Europe, or Asia. Before then, only Texas Instruments had been willing to brave the Indian bureaucracy, becoming the first multinational to establish a circuit design and development center in India in 1985. TI's center in Bangalore had its own satellite downlink but had to suffer through having an Indian government official to oversee it – with the right to examine any piece of data going in or out. Singh loosened all those reins[191] post-1991. A short time later, in 1994, HealthScribe India, a company originally funded in part by Indian-American doctors, was set up in Bangalore to do outsourced medical transcription for American doctors and hospitals. Those doctors at the time were taking handwritten notes and then dictating them into a Dictaphone for a secretary or someone

[188] exec (colloquial): executive, a person with an important managerial position in a company
[189] to sink roots (fig.) to establish a home or business somewhere
[190] to amend: to make small changes
[191] reins: (here): restrictions

else to transcribe, which would usually take days or weeks. HealthScribe set up a system that turned a doctor's touch-tone phone into a dictation machine. The doctor would punch in a number and simply dictate his notes to a PC with a voice card in it, which would digitize his voice. He could be sitting anywhere when he did it. Thanks to the satellite, a housewife or student in Bangalore could go into a computer and download that doctor's digitized voice and transcribe it – not in two weeks but in two hours. Then this person would zip it right back by satellite as a text file that could be put into the hospital's computer system and become part of the billing[192] file. Because of the twelve-hour time difference with India, Indians could do the transcription while the American doctors were sleeping, and the file would be ready and waiting the next morning. This was an important breakthrough for companies, because if you could safely, legally, and securely transcribe from Bangalore medical records, lab reports, and doctors' diagnoses – in one of the most litigious[193] industries in the world – a lot of other industries could think about sending some of their backroom work to be done in India as well. And they did. But it remained limited by what could be handled by satellite, where there was a voice delay. (Ironically, said Gurujot Singh Khalsa, one of the founders of HealthScribe, they initially explored having Indians in Maine – that is, American Indians – do this work, using some of the federal money earmarked[194] for the tribes to get started, but they could never get them interested enough to put the deal together.) The cost of doing the transcription in India was about one-fifth the cost per line of doing it in the United States, a difference that got a lot of people's attention.

By the late 1990s, though, Lady Luck was starting to shine on India from two directions: The fiber-optic bubble was starting to inflate, linking India with the United States, and the Y2K computer crisis – the so-called millennium bug – started gathering on the horizon. As you'll remember, the Y2K bug was a result of the fact that when computers were built, they came with internal clocks. In order to save memory space, these clocks rendered[195] dates with just six digits – two for the day, two for the month, and, you guessed it, two for the year. That meant they could go up to only 12/31/99. So when the calendar hit January 1, 2000, many older computers were poised[196] to register that not as 01/01/2000

[192] billing: having to do with bills (*Rechnungen*)
[193] litigious [lɪˈtɪdʒəs]: tending to take cases to court
[194] to earmark: to designate for a specific purpose
[195] to render: to make, to produce
[196] poised: on the point of doing s.th.

but as 01/01/00, and they would think it was 1900 all over again. It meant that a huge number of existing computers (newer ones were being made with better clocks) needed to have their internal clocks and related systems adjusted; otherwise, it was feared, they would shut down, creating a global crisis, given how many different management systems – from water to air traffic control – were computerized.

This computer remediation[197] work was a huge, tedious[198] job. Who in the world had enough software engineers to do it all? Answer: India, with all the techies[199] from all those IITs and private technical colleges and computer schools.

And so with Y2K bearing down on us, America and India started dating,[200] and that relationship became a huge flattener, because it demonstrated to so many different businesses that the combination of the PC, the Internet, and fiber-optic cable had created the possibility of a whole new form of collaboration and horizontal value creation: outsourcing. Any service, call center, business support operation, or knowledge work that could be digitized could be sourced globally to the cheapest, smartest, most efficient provider. Using fiber-optic-cable-connected workstations, Indian techies could get under the hood of your company's computers and do all the adjustments, even though they were located halfway around the world.

"[Y2K upgrading] was tedious work that was not going to give them an enormous competitive advantage," said Vivek Paul, the Wipro executive, whose company did some outsourced Y2K drudge work.[201] "So all these Western companies were incredibly challenged to find someone else who would do it and do it for as little money as possible. They said, 'We just want to get past the damn year 2000!' So they started to work with Indian [technology] companies who they might not have worked with otherwise."

To use my parlance,[202] they were ready to go on a blind date[203] with India. They were ready to get "fixed up." Added Jerry Rao, "Y2K means different things to different people. For Indian industry, it represented the biggest opportunity. India was considered as a place of backward

[197] remediation: repair
[198] tedious ['ti:diəs]: boring
[199] techy (colloquial): person obsessively interested in or working with information technology
[200] dating: (here): beginning to work together
[201] drudge work: monotonous work
[202] parlance: way of speaking
[203] blind date: a meeting with s.o. you have never met

people. Y2K suddenly required that every single computer in the world needed to be reviewed. And the sheer[204] number of people needed to review line-by-line code existed in India. The Indian IT industry got its footprint[205] across the globe because of Y2K. Y2K became our engine of growth, our engine of being known around the world. We never looked back after Y2K."

By early 2000, the Y2K work started to wind down, but then a whole new driver of business emerged – e-commerce. The dot-com bubble had not yet burst, engineering talent was scarce, and demand from dot-coms was enormous. Said Paul, "People wanted what they felt were mission-critical applications,[206] key to their very existence, to be done, and they could go nowhere else. So they turned to the Indian companies, and as they turned to the Indian companies they found that they were getting delivery of complex systems, with great quality, sometimes better than what they were getting from others. That created an enormous respect for Indian IT providers. And if [Y2K work] was the acquaintanceship process,[207] this was the falling-in-love process."

Outsourcing from America to India, as a new form of collaboration, exploded. By just stringing a fiber-optic line from a workstation in Bangalore to my company's mainframe, I could have Indian IT firms like Wipro, Infosys, and Tata Consulting Services managing my e-commerce and mainframe applications.

"Once we're in the mainframe business and once we're in e-commerce – now we're married," said Paul. But again, India was lucky that it could exploit all that undersea fiber-optic cable. "I had an office very close to the Leela Palace hotel in Bangalore," Paul added. "I was working with a factory located in the information technology park in Whitefield, a suburb of Bangalore, and I *could not get a local telephone line between our office and the factory.* Unless you paid a bribe, you could not get a line, and we wouldn't pay. So my phone call to Whitefield would go from my office in Bangalore to Kentucky, where there was a GE mainframe computer we were working with, and then from Kentucky to Whitefield. We used our own fiber-optic lease[208] line that ran across the ocean – but the one across town required a bribe."

---

[204] sheer: utter
[205] footprint: (here): reputation
[206] mission-critical application: software designed for a specific purpose
[207] acquaintanceship process: the process of getting to know s.o.
[208] lease: an agreement that allows you to use s.th. for a period of time in return for rent

India didn't benefit only from the dot-com boom; it benefited even more from the dot-com bust![209] That is the real irony. The boom laid the cable that connected India to the world, and the bust made the cost of using it virtually free and also vastly increased the number of American companies that would want to use that fiber-optic cable to outsource knowledge work to India.

Y2K led to this mad rush for Indian brainpower to get the programming work done. The Indian companies were good and cheap, but price wasn't first on customers' minds – getting the work done was, and India was the only place with the volume of workers to do it. Then the dot-com boom comes along right in the wake of[210] Y2K, and India is one of the few places where you can find surplus English-speaking engineers, at any price, because all of those in America have been scooped up[211] by e-commerce companies. Then the dot-com bubble bursts, the stock market tanks,[212] and the pool of investment capital dries up. American IT companies that survived the boom and venture capital[213] firms that still wanted to fund start-ups had much less cash to spend. Now they needed those Indian engineers not just because there were a lot of them, but precisely because they were low-cost. So the relationship between India and the American business community intensified another notch.[214]

One of the great mistakes made by many analysts in the early 2000s was conflating[215] the dot-com boom with globalization, suggesting that both were just fads and hot air. When the dot-com bust came along, these same wrongheaded analysts assumed that globalization was over as well. Exactly the opposite was true. The dot-com bubble was only one aspect of globalization, and when it imploded, rather than imploding globalization, it actually turbocharged it.

Promod Haque, an Indian American and one of the most prominent venture capitalists in Silicon Valley with his firm Norwest Venture Partners, was in the middle of this transition. "When the bust took place, a lot of these Indian engineers in the U.S. [on temporary work visas] got laid off, so they went back to India," explained Haque. But as a result of the bust, the IT budgets of virtually every major U.S. firm got slashed.[216]

---

[209] bust: collapse
[210] in the wake of: immediately following
[211] to scoop up (fig.): to hire
[212] to tank (colloquial): to crash
[213] venture capital: money which investors lend to start up new companies
[214] notch: level
[215] to conflate: to put together
[216] to slash: (here): to radically reduce

"Every IT manager was told to get the same amount of work or more done with less money. So guess what he does? He says, 'You remember Vijay from India who used to work here during the boom and then went back home? Let me call him over in Bangalore and see if he will do the work for us for less money than what we would pay an engineer here in the U.S.'" And thanks to all that fiber cable laid during the boom, it was easy to find Vijay and put him to work.

The Y2K computer readjustment work was done largely by low-skilled Indian programmers right out of tech schools, said Haque, "but the guys on visas who were coming to America were not trade school guys. They were guys with advanced engineering degrees. So a lot of our companies saw that these guys were good at Java and C++[217] and architectural design work for computers, and then they got laid off and went back home, and the IT manager back here who is told, 'I don't care how you get the job done, just get it done for less money,' calls Vijay." Once America and India were dating, the burgeoning[218] Indian IT companies in Bangalore started coming up with their own proposals. The Y2K work had allowed them to interact with some pretty large companies in the United States, and as a result they began to understand the pain points[219] and how to do business-process implementation[220] and improvement. So the Indians, who were doing a lot of very specific custom[221] code maintenance to higher-value-add companies, started to develop their own products and transform themselves from maintenance to product companies, offering a range of software services and consulting. This took Indian companies much deeper inside American ones, and business-process outsourcing – letting Indians run your back room – went to a whole new level. "I have an accounts payable[222] department and I could move this whole thing to India under Wipro or Infosys and cut my costs in half," said Haque. All across America, CEOs[223] were saying, "'Make it work for less,'" he added. "And the Indian companies were saying, 'I have taken a look under your hood and I will provide you with a total solution for the lowest price.'" In other words, the Indian outsourcing companies said, "Do you remember how I fixed your tires and your pistons[224] during Y2K?

[217] Java and C++: programming languages
[218] to burgeon ['bɜ:dʒn]: to begin to grow rapidly
[219] pain point (colloquial): weakness
[220] implementation: the act of carrying s.th. out
[221] custom: *maßgeschneidert*
[222] accounts payable: money that must be paid to another company
[223] CEO: chief executive office, the most important manager of a company
[224] piston: *Kolbe*

Well, I could actually give you a whole lube job[225] if you like. And now that you know me and trust me, you know I can do it." To their credit, the Indians were not just cheap, they were also hungry and ready to learn anything.

The scarcity of capital after the dot-com bust made venture capital firms see to it that the companies they were investing in were finding the most efficient, high-quality, low-price way to innovate. In the boom times, said Haque, it was not uncommon for a $50 million investment in a startup to return $500 million once the company went public.[226] After the bust, that same company's public offering might bring in only $100 million. Therefore, venture firms wanted to risk only $20 million to get that company from start-up to IPO.[227]

"For venture firms," said Haque, "the big question became, How do I get my entrepreneurs and their new companies to a point where they are breaking even or profitable sooner, so they can stop being a draw[228] on my capital and be sold so our firm can *generate good liquidity*[229] *and returns*? The answer many firms came up with was: I better start outsourcing as many functions as I can from the beginning. I have to make money for my investors faster, so what can be outsourced must be outsourced."

Henry Schacht, who was heading Lucent[230] during part of this period, saw the whole process from the side of corporate management. The business economics, he told me, became "very ugly" for everyone. Everyone found prices flat to declining and markets stagnant,[231] yet they were still spending huge amounts of money running the backroom operations of their companies, which they could no longer afford. "Cost pressures were enormous," he recalled, "and the flat world was available, [so] economics were forcing people to do things they never thought they would do or could do ... Globalization got supercharged" – for both knowledge work and manufacturing. Companies found that they could go to MIT[232] and find four incredibly smart Chinese engineers who were ready to go back to China and work for them from there for the same amount that it would cost them to hire one engineer in America. Bell Labs[233] had a

[225] lube job (colloquial): oil change
[226] to go public: to list the company on the stock market
[227] IPO: initial public offering, the first time a company is listed on the stock market
[228] draw: (here): causing a loss of profit
[229] liquidity: the ability of s.th. to be sold and thus turned into cash
[230] Lucent ['lu:sənt]: a techology company until 2006
[231] stagnant: not moving
[232] MIT: elite research university in Cambridge, Massachusetts
[233] Bell Labs: a research and development organization in New Jersey, USA

research facility at Tsingdao that could connect to Lucent's computers in America. "They would use our computers overnight," said Schacht. "Not only was the incremental[234] computing cost close to zero, but so too was the transmission cost, and the computer was idle[235] [at night]."

For all these reasons I believe that Y2K should be a national holiday in India, a second Indian Independence Day, in addition to August 15. As Johns Hopkins[236] foreign policy expert Michael Mandelbaum, who spent part of his youth in India, put it, 'Y2K should be called Indian Interdependence Day," because it was India's ability to collaborate with Western companies, thanks to the interdependence created by fiber-optic networks, that really vaulted[237] it forward and gave more Indians than ever some real freedom of choice in how, for whom, and where they worked.

To put it another way, August 15 commemorates[238] freedom at midnight. Y2K made possible *employment* at midnight – but not any employment, employment for India's best knowledge workers. August 15 gave independence to *India.* But Y2K gave independence to *Indians* – not all, by any stretch of the imagination, but a lot more than fifty years ago, and many of them from the most productive segment of the population. In that sense, yes, India was lucky, but it also reaped[239] what it had sowed[240] through hard work and education and the wisdom of its elders who built all those IITs.

Louis Pasteur said it a long time ago: "Fortune favors the prepared mind."

Flattener # 7: Supply-chaining

Eating Sushi in Arkansas

I had never seen what a supply chain looked like in action until I visited Wal-Mart headquarters in Bentonville, Arkansas. My Wal-Mart hosts took me over to the 1.2-million-square-foot distribution center, where we climbed up to a viewing perch[241] and watched the show. On one side

[234] incremental: increasing in amount
[235] idle: not in use
[236] Johns Hopkins: elite research university in Baltimore, Maryland
[237] to vault (fig.): to cause s.th. to quickly move over a large distance
[238] to commemorate: to celebrate an anniversary
[239] to reap: to harvest
[240] to sow [səʊ], sowed, sown: to plant, to place seeds in the ground
[241] perch: platform

"A Japanese company will deliver them to us for £6,75 a thousand."

of the building, scores[242] of white Wal-Mart trailer trucks[243] were dropping off boxes of merchandise from thousands of different suppliers. Boxes large and small were fed up a conveyor belt at each loading dock. These little conveyor belts fed into a bigger belt, like streams feeding into a powerful river. Twenty-four hours a day, seven days a week, the suppliers' trucks feed the twelve miles of conveyor streams, and the conveyor streams feed into a huge Wal-Mart river of boxed products. But that is just half the show. As the Wal-Mart river flows along, an electric eye reads the bar codes on each box on its way to the other side of the building. There, the river parts again into a hundred streams. Electric arms from each stream reach out and guide the boxes – ordered by particular Wal-Mart stores – off the main river and down its stream, where another conveyor belt sweeps them into a waiting Wal-Mart truck, which will rush these particular products onto the shelves of a particular Wal-Mart store somewhere in the country. There, a consumer will lift one of these products off the shelf, and the cashier will scan it in, and the moment that happens, a signal will be generated. That signal will go out

[242] scores: large numbers
[243] trailer-truck (AE): a truck that pulls a separate, long section in which goods are transported

across the Wal-Mart network to the supplier of that product – whether that supplier's factory is in coastal China or coastal Maine. That signal will pop up on the supplier's computer screen and prompt him to make another of that item and ship it via the Wal-Mart supply chain, and the whole cycle will start anew. So no sooner does your arm lift a product off the local Wal-Mart's shelf and onto the checkout counter than another mechanical arm starts making another one somewhere in the world. Call it "the Wal-Mart Symphony" in multiple movements – with no finale. It just plays over and over 24/7/365: delivery, sorting, packing, distribution, buying, manufacturing, reordering, delivery, sorting, packing ...

Just one company, Hewlett-Packard, will sell four hundred thousand computers through the four thousand Wal-Mart stores worldwide in *one day* during the Christmas season, which will require HP to adjust its supply chain, to make sure that all of its standards interface with Wal-Mart's, so that these computers flow smoothly into the Wal-Mart river, into the Wal-Mart streams, into the Wal-Mart stores.

Wal-Mart's ability to bring off[244] this symphony on a global scale – moving 2.3 billion general merchandise cartons a year down its supply chain into its stores – has made it the most important example of the next great flattener I want to discuss, which I call supply-chaining. Supply-chaining is a method of collaborating horizontally – among suppliers, retailers, and customers – to create value. Supply-chaining is both enabled by the flattening of the world and a hugely important flattener itself, because the more these supply chains grow and proliferate,[245] the more they force the adoption of common standards between companies (so that every link of every supply chain can interface with the next), the more they eliminate points of friction at borders, the more the efficiencies of one company get adopted by the others, and the more they encourage global collaboration.

To appreciate how important supply-chaining has become as a source of competitive advantage and profit in a flat world, think about this one fact: Wal-Mart today is the biggest retail company in the world, and it does not make a single thing. All it "makes" is a hyperefficient supply chain. As Yossi Sheffi, an expert on supply-chain management and a professor of engineering systems at MIT, likes to say, "Making stuff[246] – that's easy. Supply chain, now that is really hard." What he means is that with today's technology it is difficult to keep intellectual property

[244] to bring off: to accomplish
[245] to proliferate: to increase in number
[246] stuff (colloquial): term for unspecified material or things

secret and thus easy to reverse-engineer any product and "make stuff" in a matter of days. However, building a process that "delivers stuff" across the globe – involving dozens of suppliers, distributors, port operators, customs brokers,[247] forwarders, and carriers in a finely tuned chain operating in concert – is not only difficult, it's very, very hard to duplicate.

Before looking at Wal-Mart in detail, let me make a few general points about supply chains and why they have become so important. When the world is flat, your company both can and must take advantage of the best producers at the lowest prices anywhere they can be found. If you don't, your competitors will. So global supply chains – that draw parts and products from every corner of the world – have become essential for both retailers and manufacturers. That is the good news. The bad news, as Sheffi suggests, is that making these chains work is much harder than it looks and requires constant innovation and constant adjustment. There are two basic challenges in developing a global supply chain in a flat world, he explains. One is "global optimization." What that means is that it doesn't matter if you can get one part cheaper in one place. The key is that the total cost of delivering all your parts on time from all four corners of the globe to your factories or retail outlets has to be low, and certainly lower than those of your competitors.[248] "If I am the transportation manager in a company, I want to do business with the cheapest trucking company," said Sheffi. "If I am the production manager in that company, I want to do business with the most reliable trucking company. And they may not be the same." So the first challenge is balancing out all these factors to get the most reliable, low-cost delivery system in place. The second major challenge, said Sheffi, is coordinating disruption-prone[249] supply with hard-to-predict demand. That is, you don't want to buy too many of one part, or one sweater – because then you will have to discount them when they pile up on the shelves of your factory or store. But you don't want to buy too few of that part or those sweaters, either, because customers might not find what they want when they go shopping, and you may lose not only a sale that day but a customer for life. Both challenges are exacerbated[250] by the short life cycle of products today, particularly fashion and consumer electronics products. Innovation is happening much faster, and so products go in

[247] customs broker: a person who arranges for the quick import and export of goods at the border
[248] competitor: rival
[249] prone: tending toward
[250] to exacerbate: to make worse

and out of fashion much faster, which makes forecasting demand much more difficult.

There are many ways that companies try to meet these challenges, noted Sheffi. One is by replacing inventory[251] with information. This is an area that Wal-Mart pioneered. The faster you can get information from stores about what customers are buying – what products, what models, and what colors – the faster you can get that information to your manufacturers and designers and the faster they can send back down the supply chain more red sweaters and fewer yellow ones. Advanced information technology also gives Wal-Mart "visibility" into where products are at any time as they move through the supply chain. Thus, if demand is high in Texas and lower than expected in New England, Wal-Mart can redirect the flow midstream in order to ensure that products are routed to Texas, where customers want them. The Spanish fashion retailer Zara is particularly adept at this and regularly outperforms[252] its competition. Zara lives by the motto that it is more profitable to incur[253] shortages than overstock, and then to respond to shortages with lightning speed so you are offering customers exactly what they want with much less risk of leftovers. How do they do this?

Zara spends heavily on sophisticated[254] information technology, "including PDA's[255] with transmission capabilities for all store managers to monitor customer preferences and then send data directly to a central planning office," according to *Longitudes 04*, a collaborative study by Harvard Business School and UPS.[256] "This technology has so reduced execution time that it can get a new product from design to store shelves in no more than 30 days, allowing Zara to postpone design decisions to incorporate up-to-the-minute results from its stores. By planning well to handle the day-to-day risk of fickle[257] consumer tastes and rapidly changing style preferences, Zara is also prepared to adapt when unforeseen[258] events occur. Immediately after September 11, Zara executives realized that consumers were in a somber mood, and within just a few weeks [Zara executives] had stocked their stores with new merchandise that was predominantly black."

[251] inventory: all products at hand at the moment
[252] to outperform: to do better than others
[253] to incur: to allow to happen
[254] sophisticated: complex
[255] PDA's: personal data assistant, or a palm top computer
[256] UPS: United Parcel Service, a private, international postal service
[257] fickle: indecisive
[258] unforeseen: not seen in advance

This strategy is known in the business as "postponement," and the idea, explained Sheffi, whose latest work is *The Resilient*[259] *Enterprise: Overcoming Vulnerability*[260] *for Competitive Advantage*, is that as it becomes harder and harder to forecast demand, good companies find ways to postpone adding value to their products until the last possible moment. This is the genius of Dell. Because Dell has a customer for every computer before it is manufactured, Dell makes exactly the number of computers that customers want, each one exactly the way the customer wants it. It has no inventory of computers. It has a basic supply of parts and then adds value by tailoring screen size, memory, and software to the desires of each customer. "Dell can get stuck with parts that it bought on spec,[261] but each part can be used in many configurations so it is likely to be used sooner or later," said Sheffi. "Dell can never get stuck, however, with computers that don't get bought." The bottom line, concluded Sheffi, is that in a flat world, products are turned from innovations into commodities faster than ever, competition is coming from all over the globe and is more intense than ever, and consumer demand is more volatile[262] and informed than ever, with fads moving in and out around the globe like lightning bolts. In this world, a smart and fast global supply chain is becoming one of the most important ways for a company to distinguish itself from its competitors.

As consumers, we love supply chains, because they deliver us all sorts of goods – from tennis shoes to laptop computers – at lower and lower prices and tailored more and more precisely to just what we want. That is how Wal-Mart became the world's biggest retailer. But as workers, we are sometimes ambivalent or hostile to these supply chains, because they expose us to higher and higher pressures to compete, and force our companies to cut costs, and also, at times, cut our wages and benefits. That is how Wal-Mart became one of the world's most controversial companies. No retail company has been more efficient at improving its supply chain (and thereby flattening the world) than Wal-Mart, and no company epitomizes[263] the tension that supply chains evoke[264] between the consumer in us and the worker in us than does Wal-Mart. A September 30, 2002,

[259] resilient: able to adjust quickly
[260] vulnerability: weakness (*Verwundbarkeit*)
[261] spec: speculation
[262] volatile: changing suddenly
[263] to epitomize: to represent a typical example
[264] to evoke: to create, to bring about

article in *Computerworld* summed up Wal-Mart's pivotal[265] role: "'Being a supplier to Wal-Mart is a two-edged sword,' says Joseph F. Eckroth Jr., CIO at Mattel Inc. 'They're a phenomenal channel[266] but a tough customer. They demand excellence.' It's a lesson that the El Segundo, Calif.-based toy manufacturer and thousands of other suppliers learned as the world's largest retailer, Wal-Mart Stores Inc., built an inventory and supply chain management system that changed the face of business. By investing early and heavily in cutting-edge[267] technology to identify and track sales on the individual item level, the Bentonville, Ark.-based retail giant made its IT infrastructure a key competitive advantage that has been studied and copied by companies around the world. 'We view Wal-Mart as the best supply chain operator of all time,' says Pete Abell, retail research director at high-tech consultancy AMR Research Inc. in Boston."

In pursuit of the world's most efficient supply chain, Wal-Mart has piled up a list of business offenses over the years that has given the company several deserved black eyes and that it is belatedly[268] starting to address in a meaningful way. But its role as one of the ten forces that flattened the world is undeniable, and it was to get a handle on this that I decided to make my own pilgrimage to Bentonville. I don't know why, but on the flight in from La Guardia,[269] I was thinking, Boy, I would really like some sushi tonight. But where am I going to find sushi in northwest Arkansas? And even if I found it, would I want to eat it? Could you really trust the eel in Arkansas?

When I arrived at the Hilton near Wal-Mart's headquarters, I was stunned[270] to see, like a mirage, a huge Japanese steak house-sushi restaurant right next door. When I remarked to the desk clerk who was checking me in that I never expected to get my sushi fix[271] in Bentonville, he told me, "We've got three more Japanese restaurants opening up soon."

Multiple Japanese restaurants in Bentonville?

The demand for sushi in Arkansas is not an accident. It has to do with the fact that all around Wal-Mart's offices, vendors[272] have set up their own operations to be close to the mother ship. Indeed, the area is known as "Vendorville." The amazing thing about Wal-Mart's headquarters is

[265] pivotal: extremely important
[266] channel.: (here): company
[267] cutting edge (colloquial): the latest
[268] belatedly: later than it should be
[269] La Guardia: second-largest airport in New York City
[270] to stun: to surprise
[271] to get your fix (colloquial): to satisfy a great desire
[272] vendor: small businessman

that it is so, well, Wal-Mart. The corporate offices are crammed into a reconfigured warehouse. As we passed a large building made of corrugated metal, I figured it was the maintenance shed. "Those are our international offices," said my host, spokesman William Wertz. The corporate suites are housed in offices that are one notch[273] below those of the principal, vice principal, and head counselor at my daughter's public junior high school – *before it was remodeled.* When you pass through the lobby, you see these little cubicles where potential suppliers are pitching[274] their products to Wal-Mart buyers. One has sewing machines all over the table, another has dolls, another has women's shirts. It feels like a cross between Sam's Club[275] and the covered bazaar of Damascus. Attention Wal-Mart shareholders: The company is definitely not wasting your money on frills.[276]

But how did so much innovative thinking – thinking that has reshaped the world's business landscape in many ways – come out of such a Li'l Abner backwater?[277] It is actually a classic example of a phenomenon I point to often in this book: the coefficient of flatness. The fewer natural resources your country or company has, the more you will dig inside yourself for innovations in order to survive. Wal-Mart became the biggest retailer in the world because it drove a hard bargain[278] with everyone it came in contact with. But make no mistake about one thing: Wal-Mart also became number one because this little hick[279] company from northwest Arkansas was smarter and faster about adopting new technology than any of its competitors. And it still is.

David Glass, the company's CEO from 1988 to 2000, oversaw many of the innovations that made Wal-Mart the biggest and most profitable retailer on the planet. *Fortune* magazine once dubbed[280] him "the most underrated CEO ever" for the quiet way he built on Sam Walton's vision. David Glass is to supply-chaining what Bill Gates is to word processing. When Wal-Mart was just getting started in northern Arkansas in the

[273] one notch: one level or step
[274] to pitch (colloquial): to use arguments to get s.o. to buy your product
[275] Sam's Club: a chain of stores owned by Wal-Mart that sells to members only, who buy products in large quantities
[276] frill: unnecessary luxury
[277] Li'l Abner backwater: an uneventful place such as the one portrayed in the comic strip Li'l Abner
[278] to drive a hard bargain (colloquial): to negotiate so as to get what you want
[279] hick: provincial
[280] to dub: to give s.o. or s.th. a particular name

1960s, explained Glass, it wanted to be a discounter. But in those days, every five-and-dime[281] got its goods from the same wholesalers, so there was no way to get an edge on[282] your competitors. The only way Wal-Mart could see to get an edge, he said, was for it to buy its goods in volume *directly from the manufacturers.* But it wasn't efficient for manufacturers to ship to multiple Wal-Mart stores spread all over, so Wal-Mart set up a distribution center to which all the manufacturers could ship their merchandise, and then Wal-Mart got its own trucks to distribute these goods itself to its stores. The math worked like this: It cost roughly 3 percent more on average for Wal-Mart to maintain its own distribution center. But it turned out, said Glass, that cutting out the wholesalers and buying direct from the manufacturers saved on average 5 percent, so that allowed Wal-Mart to cut costs on average 2 percent and then make it up on volume.

Once it established that basic method of buying directly from manufacturers to get the deepest discounts possible, Wal-Mart focused relentlessly[283] on three things. The first was working with the manufacturers to get them to cut their costs as much as possible. The second was working on its supply chain from those manufacturers, wherever they were in the world, to Wal-Mart's distribution centers, to make it as low-cost and frictionless as possible. The third was constantly improving Wal-Mart's information systems, so it knew exactly what its customers were buying and could feed that information to all the manufacturers, so the shelves would always be stocked with the right items at the right time.

Wal-Mart quickly realized that if it could save money by buying directly from the manufacturers, by constantly innovating to cut the cost of running its supply chain, and by keeping its inventories low by learning more about its customers, it could beat its competitors on price every time. Sitting in Bentonville, Arkansas, it didn't have much choice.

"The reason we built all our own logistics and systems is because we are in the middle of nowhere," said Jay Alien, Wal-Mart's senior vice president of corporate affairs. "It really was a small town. If you wanted to go to a third party for logistics, it was impossible. It was pure survival. Now with all the attention we are getting there is an assumption that our low prices derive from our size or because we're getting stuff from China or being able to dictate to suppliers. The fact is the low prices are derived from efficiencies Wal-Mart has invested in – the system and the culture.

[281] five-and-dime: small discount store
[282] to get an edge on: to obtain an advantage over s.o.
[283] relentlessly: without any decrease of intensity

It is a very low-cost culture." Added Glass, "I wish that I could say we were brilliant and visionary, [but] it was all born out of necessity."

The more that supply chain grew, the more Walton and Glass understood that scale and efficiency were the keys to their whole business. Put simply, the more scale and scope[284] their supply chain had, the more things they sold for less to more customers, the more leverage[285] they had with suppliers to drive prices down even more, the more they sold to more customers, the more scale and scope their supply chain had, the more profit they reaped for their shareholders ...

Sam Walton was the father of that culture, but necessity was its mother, and its offspring has turned out to be a lean,[286] mean[287] supply-chain machine. In 2004, Wal-Mart purchased roughly $260 billion worth of merchandise and ran it through a supply chain consisting of 108 distribution centers around the United States, serving the some three thousand Wal-Mart stores in America.

In the early years, "we were small – we were 4 or 5 percent of Sears and Kmart," said Glass. "If you are that small, you are vulnerable,[288] so what we wanted to do more than anything else was grow market share. We had to undersell others. If I could reduce from 3 percent to 2 percent the cost of running my distribution centers, I could reduce retail prices and grow my market share and then not be vulnerable to anyone. So any efficiency we generated we passed on to the consumer."

For instance, after the manufacturers dropped off their goods at the Wal-Mart distribution center, Wal-Mart needed to deliver those goods in small bunches[289] to each of its stores. It meant that Wal-Mart had trucks going all over America. Walton quickly realized if he connected his drivers by radios and satellites, after they dropped off at a certain Wal-Mart store, they could go a few miles down the road and pick up goods from a manufacturer so they wouldn't come back empty and so Wal-Mart could save the delivery charges from that manufacturer. A few pennies here, a few pennies there, and the result is more volume, scope, and scale.

In improving its supply chain, Wal-Mart leaves no link untouched. While I was touring the Wal-Mart distribution center in Bentonville, I noticed that some boxes were too big to go on the conveyor belts and

[284] scope: range of operation
[285] leverage: (here): ability to get a better deal
[286] lean: *schlank*
[287] mean: (here): aggressive
[288] vulnerable: easily harmed
[289] bunch: amount or group of s.th.

were being moved around on pallets by Wal-Mart employees driving special minilift trucks with headphones on. A computer tracks how many pallets each employee is plucking every hour to put onto trucks for different stores, and a computerized voice tells each of them whether he is ahead of schedule or behind schedule. "You can choose whether you want your computer voice to be a man or a woman, and you can choose English or Spanish," explained Rollin Ford, Wal-Mart's executive vice president, who oversees the supply chain and was giving me my tour.

A few years ago, these pallet drivers would get written instructions for where to pluck a certain pallet and what truck to take it to, but Wal-Mart discovered that by giving them headphones with a soothing[290] computer voice to instruct them, drivers could use both hands and not have to carry pieces of paper. And by having the voice constantly reminding them whether they were behind or ahead of expectations, "we got a boost in productivity," said Ford. It is a million tiny operational innovations like this that differentiate Wal-Mart's supply chain.

But the real breakthrough, said Glass, was when Wal-Mart realized that while it had to be a tough bargainer with its manufacturers on price, at the same time the two had to collaborate to create value for each other horizontally if Wal-Mart was going to keep driving down costs. Wal-Mart was one of the first companies to introduce computers to track store sales and inventory and was the first to develop a computerized network in order to share this information with suppliers. Wal-Mart's theory was that the more information everyone had about what customers were pulling off the shelves, the more efficient Wal-Mart's buying would be, the quicker its suppliers could adapt to changing market demand.

In 1983, Wal-Mart invested in point-of-sale terminals, which simultaneously rang up[291] sales and tracked inventory deductions[292] for rapid resupply. Four years later, it installed a large-scale satellite system linking all of the stores to company headquarters, giving Wal-Mart's central computer system real-time inventory data and paving the way for a supply chain greased by information and humming down to the last atom of efficiency. A major supplier can now tap into Wal-Mart's Retail Link private extranet system to see exactly how its products are selling and when it might need to up its production.

"'Opening its sales and inventory databases to suppliers is what made Wal-Mart the powerhouse it is today,' Rena Granofsky, a senior partner at

---

[290] to sooth: to comfort

[291] to ring up: (here): to register

[292] deduction: reduction

J.C. Williams Group Ltd., a Toronto-based retail consulting firm," said in the 2002 *Computerworld* article on Wal-Mart. "'While its competition guarded sales information, Wal-Mart approached its suppliers as if they were partners, not adversaries,'"[293] says Granofsky. By implementing a collaborative planning, forecasting, and replenishment[294] (CPFR) program, Wal-Mart began a just-in-time inventory program that reduced carrying costs for both the retailer and its suppliers. "'There's a lot less excess inventory in the supply chain because of it,' Granofsky says." Thanks to the efficiency of its supply chain alone, Wal-Mart's cost of goods is estimated[295] to be 5 to 10 percent less than that of most of its competitors.

Now Wal-Mart, in its latest supply-chain innovation, has introduced RFID–radio frequency identification microchips, attached to each pallet and merchandise box that comes into Wal-Mart, to replace bar codes, which have to be scanned individually and can get ripped or soiled.[296] In June 2003, Wal-Mart informed its top one hundred suppliers that by January 1, 2005, all pallets and boxes that they ship to Wal-Mart distribution centers have to come equipped with RFID tags. (According to the RFID *Journal*, "RFID is a generic term for technologies that use radio waves to automatically identify people or objects. There are several methods of identification, but the most common is to store a serial number that identifies a person or object, and perhaps other information, on a microchip that is attached to an antenna – the chip and the antenna together are called an RFID transponder or an RFID tag. The antenna enables the chip to transmit the identification information to a reader. The reader converts the radio waves reflected back from the RFID tag into digital information that can then be passed on to computers that can make use of it.") RFID will allow Wal-Mart to track any pallet or box at each stage in its supply chain and know exactly what product from which manufacturer is inside, with what expiration date.[297] If a grocery item[298] has to be stored at a certain temperature, the RFID tag will tell Wal-Mart when the temperature is too high or too low. Because each of these tags costs around 20¢, Wal-Mart is reserving them now for big boxes and pallets, not individual items. This is clearly the wave of the fu-

---

[293] adversary: opponent
[294] replenishment: the act of resupplying
[295] to estimate: to calculate roughly
[296] to soil: to make s.th. dirty
[297] expiration date: date at which the product is no longer useable
[298] grocery item: food item

ture. RFID technology and sophisticated order analysis tools that monitor even the most minute market activity are rapidly leading us toward industry's holy grail[299] – absolute balance in supply and demand.

"When you have RFID," said Rollin Ford, the Wal-Mart logistics vice president, "you have more insights." You can tell even faster which stores sell more of which shampoo on Fridays and which ones on Sundays, and whether Hispanics prefer to shop more on Saturday nights rather than Mondays in the stores in their neighborhoods. "When all this information is fed into our demand models, we can become more efficient on when we produce [a product] and when we ship it and then put it on the trucks in exactly the right place inside the trucks so it can flow more efficiently," added Ford. "We used to have to count each piece, and scanning it at [the receiving end] was a bottleneck.[300] Now [with RFID], we just scan the whole pallet under a bubble, and it says you have all thirty items you ordered and each box tells you, 'This is what I am and this is how I am feeling, this is what color I am, and am I in good shape' – so it makes receiving hugely easier." Procter & Gamble[301] spokesperson Jeannie Tharrington talked to Salon.com (September 20, 2004) about Wal-Mart's move to RFID: "We see this as beneficial to the entire supply chain. Right now our out-of-stock levels are higher than we'd like and certainly higher than the consumer would like, and we think this technology can help us to keep the products on the shelf more often." RFID will also allow for quicker remixing of the supply chain in response to events.

During hurricanes, Wal-Mart officials told me, Wal-Mart knows that people eat more things like Pop-Tarts[302] – easy-to-store, nonperishable[303] items – and that their stores also sell a lot of kids' games that don't require electricity and can substitute for TV. It also knows that when hurricanes are coming, people tend to drink more beer. So the minute Wal-Mart's meteorologists tell headquarters a hurricane is bearing down on Florida, its supply chain automatically adjusts to a hurricane mix in the Florida stores – more beer early, more Pop-Tarts later.

Wal-Mart is constantly looking for new ways to collaborate with its customers. Lately, it has gone into banking. It found that in areas with

---

[299] holy grail (colloquial): the thing that one is most trying to achieve
[300] bottleneck: the place where things slow down, as when two lanes of traffic have to merge
[301] Procter & Gamble: one of the largest American manufacturers of household goods
[302] Pop-Tarts®: a prepackaged breakfast pastry
[303] nonperishable: lasting for a long time

large Hispanic populations, many people had no affiliation with a bank and were getting ripped off[304] by check-cashing outlets. So Wal-Mart offered them payroll check cashing, money orders, money transfers, and even bill payment services for standard items like electricity bills – all for very small fees. Wal-Mart had an internal capability to do that for its own employees and simply turned it into an external business.

TOO MUCH OF A GOOD THING

Unfortunately for Wal-Mart, the same factors that drove its instinct for constant innovation – its isolation from the world, its need to dig inside itself, and its need to connect remote locations to a global supply chain – also got it in trouble. It is hard to exaggerate how isolated Bentonville, Arkansas, is from the currents of global debate on labor and human rights, and it is easy to see how this insular company, obsessed with lowering prices, could have gone over the edge[305] in some of its practices.

Sam Walton bred[306] not only a kind of ruthless[307] quest[308] for efficiency in improving Wal-Mart's supply chain but also a degree of ruthlessness period.[309] I am talking about everything from Wal-Mart's recently exposed practice of locking overnight workers into its stores, to its allowing Wal-Mart's maintenance contractors to use illegal immigrants as janitors, to its role as defendant in the largest civil-rights class-action lawsuit[310] in history, to its refusal to stock certain magazines – like *Playboy*[311] –on its shelves, even in small towns where Wal-Mart is the only major store. This is all aside from the fact that some of Wal-Mart's biggest competitors complain that they have had to cut health-care benefits and create a lower wage tier[312] to compete with Wal-Mart, which pays less and covers less than most big companies (more on this later). One can only hope that all the bad publicity Wal-Mart has received in the last few years will force it to understand that there is a fine line between a hyperefficient

[304] to rip off (colloquial): to cheat
[305] over the edge: too far
[306] to breed, bred, bred: (here): to create
[307] ruthless: without pity
[308] quest: search
[309] period: (here): And there is nothing to add to this!
[310] class action lawsuit: when a group of people try to be compensated for the common damages they have suffered
[311] *Playboy*: a men's magazine that features photographs of nude women as well as journalism and fiction
[312] tier: level

global supply chain that is helping people save money and improve their lives and one that has pursued cost cutting and profit margins to such a degree that whatever social benefits it is offering with one hand, it is taking away with the other.

Wal-Mart is the China of companies. It has so much leverage that it can grind down any supplier to the last halfpenny. And it is not at all hesitant about using its ability to play its foreign and domestic suppliers off against one another.

Some suppliers have found ways to flourish[313] under the pressure and become better at what they do. If all of Wal-Mart's suppliers were being squeezed dry by Wal-Mart, Wal-Mart would have no suppliers. So obviously many of them are thriving as Wal-Mart's partners. But some no doubt have translated Wal-Mart's incessant[314] price pressure into lower wages and benefits for their employees or watched as their business moved to China, whence[315] Wal-Mart's supply chain pulled in $18 billion worth of goods in 2004 from five thousand Chinese suppliers. "If Wal-Mart were an individual economy, it would rank[316] as China's eighth-biggest trading partner, ahead of Russia, Australia and Canada," Xu Jun, the spokesman for Wal-Mart China, told the *China Business Weekly* (November 29, 2004).

The successor generation to Sam Walton's leadership seems to recognize that it has both an image and a reality to fix. How far Wal-Mart will adjust remains to be seen. But when I asked Wal-Mart's CEO, H. Lee Scott Jr., directly about all these issues, he did not duck.[317] In fact, he wanted to talk about it. "What I think I have to do is institutionalize this sense of obligation to society to the same extent that we have institutionalized the commitment to the customer," said Scott. "The world has changed and we have missed that. We believed that good intentions and good stores and good prices would cause people to forgive what we are not as good at, and we were wrong." In certain areas, he added, "we are not as good as we should be. We just have to get better."

One trend that Wal-Mart insists it is not responsible for is the offshoring of manufacturing. "We are much better off if we can buy merchandise made in the United States," said Glass. "I spent two years going around this country trying to talk people into manufacturing here. We

---

[313] to flourish: (here): to be very successful
[314] incessant: continuous
[315] whence: from where
[316] to rank: to rate
[317] to duck: (here): to avoid an issue

would pay more to buy it here because the manufacturing facilities in those towns [would create jobs for] all those people who shopped in our stores. Sanyo had a plant here [in Arkansas] making television sets for Sears, and Sears cut them off, so they decided they were closing the plant and going to move part to Mexico and part to Asia. Our governor asked if we would help. We decided we would buy television sets from Sanyo [if they would keep the plant in Arkansas], and they didn't want to do it. They wanted to move it, and [the governor] even talked to the [Japanese owning] family to try to persuade them to stay. Between his efforts and ours, we persuaded them to do it. They are now the world's largest producer of televisions. We just bought our fifty millionth set from them. But for the most part people in this country have just abandoned[318] the manufacturing process. They say, 'I want to sell to you, but I don't want the responsibility for the buildings and employees [and health care]. I want to source it somewhere else.' So we were forced to source merchandise in other places in the world." He added, "One of my concerns is that, with the manufacturing out of this country, one day we'll all be selling hamburgers to each other."

The best way to get a taste of Wal-Mart's power as a global flattener is to visit Japan. Commodore Matthew Calbraith Perry opened a largely closed Japanese society to the Western world on July 8, 1853, when he arrived in Edo (Tokyo) Bay with four big black steamships bristling[319] with guns. According to the Naval Historical Center Web site, the Japanese, not knowing that steamships even existed, were shocked by the sight of them and thought they were "giant dragons puffing smoke." Commodore Perry returned a year later, and on March 31, 1854, concluded the Treaty of Kanagawa with the Japanese authorities, gaining U.S. vessels access to the ports of Shimoda and Hakodate and opening a U.S. consulate in Shimoda. This treaty led to an explosion of trade between Japan and the United States, helped open Japan to the Western world generally, and is widely credited with triggering[320] the modernization of the Japanese state, as the Japanese realized how far behind they were and rushed to catch up. And catch up they did. In so many areas, from automobiles to consumer electronics to machine tools, from the Sony Walkman to the Lexus, the Japanese learned every lesson they could from Western nations and then proceeded to beat us at our own game – except one: retailing, especially discount retailing. Japan could make those Sonys

[318] to abandon: to leave behind
[319] bristling: covered with a great number of s.th.
[320] to trigger: to start

like nobody else, but when it came to selling them at a discount, well, that was another matter.

So almost exactly 150 years after Commodore Perry signed that treaty, another lesser-known treaty was signed, actually a business partnership. Call it the Seiyu-Wal-Mart Treaty of 2003. Unlike Commodore Perry, Wal-Mart did not have to muscle its way into Japan with warships. Its reputation preceded it, which is why it was invited in by Seiyu, a struggling Japanese retail chain desperate to adapt the Wal-Mart formula in Japan, a country notorious for resisting big-box discount stores. As I traveled on the bullet train[321] from Tokyo to Numazu, site of the first Seiyu store that was using the Wal-Mart methods, the *New York Times* translator pointed out that this store was located about one hundred miles from Shimoda and that first U.S. consulate. Commodore Perry probably would have loved shopping in the new Seiyu store, where all the music piped in consists of Western tunes designed to lull shoppers into filling their carts, and where you can buy a man's suit – made in China – for $65 and a white shirt to go with it for $5. Around Wal-Mart that's called EDLP – Every Day Low Prices – and this was one of the first phrases Wal-Mart folks learned to say in Japanese.

Wal-Mart's flattening effects are fully on display in the Seiyu store in Numazu – not just the everyday low prices, but the wide aisles,[322] the big pallets of household goods, the huge signs displaying the lowest prices in each category, and the Wal-Mart supply-chain computer system so that store managers can quickly adjust stock.

I asked Seiyu's CEO, Masao Kiuchi, why he had turned to Wal-Mart. "The first time I knew about Wal-Mart was about fifteen years ago," explained Kiuchi. "I went to Dallas to see the Wal-Mart stores, and I thought this was a very rational method. It was two things: One was the signage showing the prices. It was very easy for us to understand." The second, he said, was that the Japanese thought a discount store meant that you sold cheap products at cheap prices. What he realized from shopping at Wal-Mart, and seeing everything from plasma TVs to top-brand pet products, was that Wal-Mart sold quality products at low prices.

"At the store in Dallas, I took pictures, and I brought those pictures to my colleagues in Seiyu and said, 'Look, we have to see what Wal-Mart is doing on the other side of the planet.' But showing pictures was not good enough, because how can you understand by just looking at pictures?"

321 bullet train (colloquial): high-speed train
322 aisle [aɪl]: walkway (*Gang*)

recalled Kiuchi. Eventually, Kiuchi approached Wal-Mart, and they signed a partnership on December 31, 2003. Wal-Mart bought a piece of Seiyu; in return, Wal-Mart agreed to teach Seiyu its unique form of collaboration: global supply-chaining to bring consumers the best goods at the lowest prices.

There was one big thing, though, that Seiyu had to teach Wal-Mart, Kiuchi told me: how to sell raw fish. Japanese discounters and department stores all have grocery sections, and they all carry fish for very discriminating Japanese consumers. Seiyu will discount fish several times during each day, as the freshness declines.[323]

"Wal-Mart doesn't understand raw fish," said Kiuchi. "We are expecting their help with general merchandising."

Give Wal-Mart time. I expect that in the not-too-distant future we will see Wal-Mart sushi.

Somebody had better warn the tuna.

Flattener # 9: In-Forming

Google, Yahoo!, MSN Web Search

Google headquarters in Mountain View, California, has a certain Epcot Center[324] feel to it – so many fun space-age toys to play with, so little time. In one corner is a spinning globe that emits[325] light beams based on the volume of people searching on Google. As you would expect, most of the shafts of light are shooting up from North America, Europe, Korea, Japan, and coastal China. The Middle East and Africa remain pretty dark. In another corner is a screen that shows a sample of what things people are searching for at that moment, all over the world. When I was there in 2001, I asked my hosts what had been the most frequent searches lately. One, of course, was "sex," a perennial[326] favorite of Googlers. Another was "God." Lots of people searching for Him or Her. A third was "jobs" – you can't find enough of those. And the fourth most searched item around the time of my visit? I didn't know whether to laugh or cry: "professional wrestling." The weirdest one, though, is

[323] to decline: to become less
[324] Epcot Center: Walt Disney theme park in Florida that deals with science and technology
[325] to emit: to release
[326] perennial: happening again and again

the Google recipe[327] book, where people just open their refrigerators, see what ingredients are inside, type three of them into Google, and see what recipes come up!

Fortunately, no single word or subject accounts for more than 1 or 2 percent of all Google searches at any given time, so no one should get too worried about the fate of humanity on the basis of Google's top search items on any particular day. Indeed, it is the remarkable diversity of searches going on via Google, in so many different tongues, that makes the Google search engine (and search engines in general) such huge flatteners. Never before in the history of the planet have so many people – *on their own* – had the ability to find so much information about so many things and about so many other people.

Said Russian-born Google cofounder Sergey Brin, "If someone has broadband, dial-up, or access to an Internet café, whether a kid in Cambodia, the university professor, or me who runs this search engine, all have the same basic access to overall research information that anyone has. It is a total equalizer. This is very different than how I grew up. My best access was some library, and it did not have all that much stuff, and you either had to hope for a miracle or search for something very simple or something very recent." When Google came along, he added, suddenly that kid had "universal access" to the information in libraries all over the world.

That is certainly Google's goal – to make easily available all the world's knowledge in every language. And Google hopes that in time, with a PalmPilot or a cell phone, everyone everywhere will be able to carry around access to all the world's knowledge in their pockets. "Everything" and "everyone" are key words that you hear around Google all the time. Indeed, the official Google history carried on its home page notes that the name "Google" is a play on the word "'googol,' which is the number represented by the numeral 1 followed by 100 zeros. Google's use of the term reflects the company's mission to organize the immense, seemingly infinite amount of information available on the Web," just for you. What Google's success reflects is how much people are interested in having just that – all the world's knowledge at their fingertips. There is no bigger flattener than the idea of making all the world's knowledge, or even just a big chunk of it, available to anyone and everyone, anytime, anywhere.

"We do discriminate only to the degree that if you can't use a computer or don't have access to one, you can't use Google, but other

[327] recipe ['resəpi]: instructions for making something out of particular ingredients

than that, if you can type, you can use Google," said Google CEO Eric Schmidt. And surely if the flattening of the world means anything, he added, it means that "there is no discrimination in accessing knowledge. Google is now searchable in one hundred languages, and every time we find another we increase it. Let's imagine a group with a Google iPod one day and you can tell it to search by voice – that would take care of people who can't use a computer – and then [Google access] just becomes about the rate at which we can get cheap devices[328] into people's hands."

How does searching fit into the concept of collaboration? I call it "in-forming." In-forming is the individual's personal analog to uploading, outsourcing, insourcing, supply-chaining, and offshoring. In-forming is the ability to build and deploy your own personal supply chain – a supply chain of information, knowledge, and entertainment. In-forming is about self-collaboration – becoming your own self-directed and self-empowered researcher, editor, and selector of entertainment, without having to go to the library or the movie theater or through network television. In-forming is searching for knowledge. It is about seeking like-minded people and communities. Google's phenomenal global popularity, which has spurred[329] Yahoo! and Microsoft (through its MSN Search) also to make power searching and in-forming prominent features of their Web sites, shows how hungry people are for this form of collaboration. Google is now processing roughly one billion searches per day, up from 150 million just three years ago.

The easier and more accurate searching becomes, added Larry Page, Google's other cofounder, the more global Google's user base becomes, and the more powerful a flattener it becomes. Every day more and more people are able to in-form themselves in their own language. Today, said Page, "only a third of our searches are U.S.-based, and less than half are in English." Moreover, he added, "as people are searching for more obscure things, people are publishing more obscure things," which drives the flattening effect of in-forming even more. All the major search engines have also recently added the capability for users to search not only the Web for information but also their own computer's hard drive for words or data or e-mail they know is in there somewhere but have forgotten where. When you can search your own memory more efficiently, that is really in-forming. In late 2004, Google announced plans to scan the entire contents of both the University of Michigan and Stanford

[328] device: machine (Gerät)

[329] to spur: to encourage, to induce

University libraries, making tens of thousands of books available and searchable online.

In the earliest days of search engines, people were amazed and delighted to stumble across[330] the information they sought; eureka[331] moments were unexpected surprises, said Yahoo!'s cofounder Jerry Yang. "Today their attitudes are much more presumptive. They presume[332] that the information they're looking for is certainly available and that it's just a matter of technologists making it easier to get to, and in fewer keystrokes," he said. "The democratization of information is having a profound impact on society. Today's consumers are much more efficient – they can find information, products, services, faster [through search engines] than through traditional means. They are better informed about issues related to work, health, leisure, etc. Small towns are no longer disadvantaged relative to those with better access to information. And people have the ability to be better connected to things that interest them, to quickly and easily become experts in given subjects and to connect with others who share their interests."

Google's founders understood that by the late 1990s hundreds of thousands of Web pages were being added to the Internet each day, and that existing search engines, which tended to search for keywords, could not keep pace.[333] Brin and Page, who met as Stanford University graduate students in computer science in 1995, developed a mathematical formula that ranked a Web page by how many other Web pages were linked to it, on the assumption that the more people linked to a certain page, the more important the page. The key breakthrough that enabled Google to become first among search engines was its ability to combine its PageRank technology with an analysis of page content, which determines[334] which pages are most relevant to the specific search being conducted. Even though Google entered the market after other major search players, its answers were seen by people as more accurate and relevant to what they were looking for. The fact that one search engine was just a little better than the others led a tidal wave[335] of people to switch to it. (Google now employs scores of mathematicians working on its search algorithms, in an effort to always keep them one step more relevant than the competition.)

---

[330] to stumble across: to find
[331] eureka [ju'ri:kə]: exclaimation uttered in an instance of unexpected discovery
[332] to presume: to expect
[333] to keep pace: to keep up the same speed
[334] to determine: to decide
[335] tidal wave (fig.): sudden increase

For some reason, said Brin, "people underestimated the importance of finding information, as opposed to other things you would do online. If you are searching for something like a health issue, you really want to know; in some cases it is a life-and-death matter. We have people who search Google for heart-attack symptoms and then call nine-one-one." But sometimes you really want to in-form yourself about something much simpler.

When I was in Beijing in June 2004, I was riding the elevator down one morning with my wife, Ann, and sixteen-year-old daughter, Natalie, who was carrying a fistful of postcards written to her friends. Ann said to her, "Did you bring their addresses along?" Natalie looked at her as if she were positively nineteenth-century.[336] "No," she said, with that you-are-so-out-of-it-Mom tone of voice. "I just Googled their phone numbers, and their home addresses came up."

Address book? You dummy, Mom.

All that Natalie was doing was in-forming, using Google in a way that I had no idea was possible. Thanks to Google, all that digitized information that we were creating with our PCs was suddenly searchable. It could suddenly be mined. What is staggering[337] is how much information there is out there – information that was never searchable, but will be in the future, thanks to ever smarter search engines, which will be able to sift through larger and larger mountains of different kinds of data – from pictures to videos to home listings[338] to traffic reports to high school newspapers and health cures. "People have thought about text as the one source of information," said Kai-Fu Lee, who originally set up the Microsoft research center in Beijing and now directs Google's operations in China. "But there are images, videos, books, even from ages ago, that now will be searchable. There is geographical information, maps, and there is local information and there is personal information. Information on your computer ... Basically everything we see, hear, touch, read, and write is information – and right now Internet search covers only a tiny, tiny fraction of everything that could be browsed and searched and navigated." In time, individuals will have the power to find anything in the world at any time on all kinds of devices – and that will be enormously empowering. "What excites me is the empowerment," added Lee. "I will be able to focus my time and attention and brainpower

[336] nineteenth-century: (here): old-fashioned
[337] staggering: astounding
[338] home listing: advertisement for houses that are for sale

on what I do best, which is not looking for stuff." It is building, designing, imagining, and creating stuff.

While we were traveling in China, Natalie also had her iPod with her, which empowered her to in-form herself in another way – with entertainment instead of knowledge. She had become her own music editor and loaded all her favorite songs onto her iPod and was carrying them all over China. Think about it: For decades the broadcast industry was built around the idea that you shoot out ads on network television or radio and hope that someone is watching or listening. But thanks to the flattening technologies in entertainment, that world is quickly fading away.[339] Now with TiVo you can become your own TV editor. TiVo allows viewers to digitally record their favorite programs and skip the ads, except those they want to see. You watch what you want when you want. You don't have to make an appointment[340] with a TV channel at the time and place someone else sets and watch the commercials foisted on[341] you. With TiVo you can watch only your own shows and the commercials you want for only those products in which you might be interested.

But just as Google can track what you are searching for, so too can TiVo, which knows which shows and which ads you are freezing, storing, and rewinding on your own TV. So here's a news quiz: Guess what was the most rewound moment in TV history? Answer: Janet's Jackson breast exposure,[342] or, as it was euphemistically[343] called, her "wardrobe malfunction," at the 2004 Super Bowl. Just ask TiVo. In a press release it issued on February 2, 2004, TiVo said, "Justin Timberlake and Janet Jackson stole the show during Sunday's Super Bowl, attracting almost twice as many viewers as the most thrilling[344] moments on the field, according to an annual measurement of second-by-second viewership in TiVo households. The Jackson-Timberlake moment drew the biggest spike[345] in audience reaction TiVo has ever measured. TiVo said viewership spiked up to 180 percent as hundreds of thousands of households used TiVo's unique capabilities to pause and replay live television to view the incident again and again."

---

[339] to fade away: to slowly disappear
[340] appointment: a meeting time
[341] to foist on: to force on s.o.
[342] exposure: making s.th. visible
[343] euphemistically [ˌjuːfəˈmɪstɪkli]: in a mild, indirect way
[344] thrilling: exciting
[345] spike: sharp increase

So if everyone can increasingly watch what he wants however many times he wants when he wants, the whole notion of broadcast TV – which is that we throw shows out there one time, along with their commercials, and then try to survey who is watching – will increasingly make less and less sense. The companies you want to bet on are those that, like Google or Yahoo! or TiVo, learn to collaborate with their users and offer them shows and advertisements tailored just for them. I can imagine a day soon when advertisers won't pay for anything other than that.

Companies like Google, Yahoo!, Amazon.com, and TiVo have learned to thrive[346] not by pushing products and services on their customers so much as by building collaborative systems that enable customers to pull on their own, and then responding with lightning quickness to what they pull. It is so much more efficient.

"Search is so highly personal that searching is empowering for humans like nothing else," said Google CEO Eric Schmidt. "It is the antithesis of being told or taught. It is about self-empowerment; it is empowering individuals to do what they think best with the information they want. It is very different from anything else that preceded it. Radio was one-to-many. TV was one-to-many. The telephone was one-to-one. Search is the ultimate expression of the power of the individual, using a computer, looking at the world, and finding exactly what they want – and everyone is different when it comes to that."

Of course, what made Google not just a search engine but a hugely profitable business was its founders' realization that they could build a targeted advertising model that would show you ads that are relevant to you when you searched for a specific topic and then could charge advertisers for the number of times Google users clicked on their ads. Whereas CBS broadcasts a movie and has only a rough idea who is watching it or the advertisements, Google knows exactly what you are interested in – after all, you are searching for it – and can link you up with advertisers directly or indirectly connected to your searches. In late 2004, Google began a service whereby if you are walking around Bethesda, Maryland, and are in the mood for sushi, you just send Google an SMS message on your cell phone that says "Sushi 20817" – the Bethesda zip code[347] – and it will send you back a text message of choices. Lord only knows[348] where this will go.

---

[346] to thrive: to grow strongly, to flourish
[347] zip code: *Postleitzahl*
[348] lord only knows (colloquial): It is difficult to predict.

In-forming, though, also involves searching for friends, allies, and collaborators. It is empowering the formation of global communities, across all international and cultural boundaries, which is another critically important flattening function. People can now search out fellow collaborators on any subject, project, or theme – particularly through portals like Yahoo! Groups. Yahoo! has about 300 million users and 4 million active groups. Those groups have 13 million unique individuals accessing them each month from all over the world.

"The Internet is growing in the self-services area, and Yahoo! Groups exemplifies this trend," said Jerry Yang. "It provides a forum, a platform, a set of tools for people to have private, semiprivate, or public gatherings on the Internet regardless of geography or time. It enables consumers to gather around topics that are meaningful to them in ways that are either impractical or impossible offline. Groups can serve as support groups for complete strangers who are galvanized[349] by a common issue (coping with[350] rare diseases, first-time parents, spouses of active-duty personnel[351]) or who seek others who share similar interests (hobbies as esoteric as dog-sledding, blackjack, and indoor tanning have large memberships). Existing communities can migrate online and flourish in an interactive environment (local kids' soccer league, church youth group, alumni organizations), providing a virtual home for groups interested in sharing, organizing, and communicating information valuable to cultivating vibrant[352] communities. Some groups exist only online and could never be as successful offline, while others mirror strong real-world communities. Groups can be created instantaneously and dissolved; topics can change or stay constant. This trend will only grow as consumers increasingly become publishers, and they can seek the affinity[353] and community *they* choose – when, where, and how they choose it."

When individuals are empowered to inform themselves in all these new ways, it is enormously flattening – but also enormously frightening. Why? Because people will be able to drill[354] down for information about you and me that used to be either impossible or very difficult to locate. Our lives and our pasts used to have rock-hard cement floors under them. It took a lot to drill through those floors and even then it was often hard

[349] to galvanize: to excite
[350] to cope with: to deal with s.o. or s.th.
[351] active-duty personnel: people serving in the military who are currently stationed away from home
[352] vibrant: lively
[353] affinity: similar interest
[354] to drill: *bohren*

to find out what was really down there. Yes, those hard floors sometimes protected bad people – from con men[355] to pedophiles – as they moved from town to town. But they also protected you and me and our basic privacy, making it difficult for prying[356] strangers to dig too deeply into our past or present. But Google, Yahoo!, and MSN Search are getting rid of those hard floors, very quickly, so anyone can drill into anyone else's past with a few thumb clicks on a PalmPilot. You never know anymore what kind of electronic footprints you are leaving in databases that you assume are private and will now, or soon will be, searchable. And you may be shocked to discover all the things that people, or companies, can find out about you – from your salary to where you live to your favorite books – just by Googling you.

Everyone can now be Googled – but everyone now can also Google. Google also equalizes access to information – it has no class boundaries, few education boundaries, few linguistic boundaries, and virtually no money boundaries. If you can get on Google, you have access to the world's greatest research tool, without having to go to MIT. "If I can operate Google, I can find anything," said Alan Cohen, then vice president of Airespace, which sells wireless technology. "Google is like God. God is wireless, God is everywhere, and God sees everything. Any questions in the world, you ask Google."

[355] con man: *Betrüger, Hochstapler*
[356] to pry: to try to get personal information in a way that is annoying

Chapter 12: Globalization of the Local

The Cultural Revolution Is About to Begin

My 1999 book *The Lexus and the Olive Tree* attempted to describe the forces that were globalizing the world at the end of the twentieth century and their effects on economics, politics, geopolitics, environment, and culture. After the first edition of *The World Is Flat* first came out, several readers complained to me that I had not followed up on the cultural part of my argument in *The Lexus and the Olive Tree* – I had made no mention of how this new flattening era of globalization, at the dawn of the twenty-first century, was affecting culture around the world. I acknowledged this and explained that it was simply a matter of not having had enough time to think through that issue. This updated edition of the book has given me a chance to do just that, and I am glad it has, because the flattening of the world is having surprising, important, and paradoxical effects on culture around the world.

As the flattening phase of globalization began to gain momentum following the fall of the Berlin Wall, there was a considerable[357] and justifiable[358] worry around the world that "globalization means Americanization." This worry was not unreasonable, because it was primarily American-based manufacturers and service providers, American brands and American moviemakers, American singers and American entertainers, American clothing designers and American fast-food chains that were in the best position to take advantage of the falling of the walls and flattening of the world. They were the first out of the gates, and it seemed inevitable and unstoppable that they would take advantage of the flat world to homogenize culture. If you were from another culture, no matter how robust and vibrant your distinctive dress, language, food, or music, you had to worry that you could be easily steam rolled.[359] In the constant struggle between the homogenizing and particularizing forces of globalization, it seemed like the homogenizing-Americanizing forces were destined to triumph. Globalization would have an American face, an American look, and an American taste.

---

[357] considerable: significant

[358] to justify: to show that something is just or right

[359] to steam roll (fig.): to defeat s.o. or force this person to do s.th. because you have more power or authority

This naturally triggered a backlash against globalization as a form of "American cultural imperialism." Many people around the world argued that unless we took serious steps to strengthen cultures – and protect the environment – the juggernaut[360] of globalization as Americanization could, in just a few decades, wipe out the cultural, ecological, and zoological diversity that took millions of years of human, plant, and animal evolution to produce.

There is no minimizing the dangers posed[361] to the environment by the flattening of the world, as I explained in the previous chapter. However, as far as culture is concerned, there is reason to hope that the flattening of the world will not necessarily pave the way for a red, white, and blue cultural homogenization. Indeed, it is becoming clear that the flat-world platform, while it has the potential to homogenize cultures, also has, I would argue, an even greater potential to nourish[362] diversity to a degree that the world has never seen before.

Why? Primarily because of uploading. Uploading makes possible "the globalization of the local." The fact that so many people worldwide now have the tools to create and upload their own content – their own news reports, their own opinions, their own music, their own videos, their own photos, their own software, their own encyclopedias, their own dictionaries – is a very powerful force for the preservation and enhancement[363] of cultural autonomy and particularity. The flat-world platform enables you to take your own local culture and upload it to the world. It means you aren't stuck downloading Mickey Mouse and McDonald's. No, no, no. You can now write your own song, create a podcast version in any language you like, and share it with the world on some podcast site, and if people like it, it will spread. You can now make your own home video with a cheap Webcam and Microsoft Movie Maker that comes bundled with your software and upload that as well. The most popular food in the world is not the Big Mac. It's pizza. And what is pizza? It is just a flat piece of dough[364] on which every culture puts its own distinctive foods and flavors. So Japan has sushi pizza and Bangkok has Thai pizza and Lebanon has meze[365] pizza. The flat-world platform is just like that pizza

[360] juggernaut: a great force
[361] to pose: to present
[362] to nourish: to promote
[363] enhancement: increase in value or quality
[364] dough ['dəʊ]: *Teig*
[365] meze ['mezeɪ]: assorted Arabian appetizers

dough. It allows different cultures to season and flavor it as they like – and you are going to see that more now than ever.

At the same time, the fact that people in rising nations like India and China will be able to innovate without having to emigrate means that local cultures have a much better chance of being preserved.[366] A young Indian engineer no longer has to stand in line outside the U.S. embassy in New Delhi and pray to win the lottery and secure a visa to America so that he or she can move to frigid[367] Minnesota and give up his or her native dress, native cuisine, native music, and extended family – all the things that make up a native culture – just to get a decent engineering job at 3M.[368] That is a very good thing for the preservation of Indian local culture. Cultures are nested in environments, and the fact that more people can now not only survive but even thrive by staying home in their native region, in their own environment, has got to be a net plus for the forces of cultural diversity versus the forces of homogeneity.

Moreover, even those individuals who have had to uproot themselves[369] from developing countries to go west – to Europe or America in particular – have been able to take advantage of the flattening of the world to hold on to many aspects of their local culture, even if they are living in the midst of a different one thousands of miles away. Thanks to their ability to read their local newspapers online, to communicate with family and friends by phone for almost nothing using voice over the Internet technology, to watch daily news from Cairo or Calcutta (in Arabic and Hindi) thanks to Internet or satellite TV, the forces of particularization now seem to be as strong as the forces of homogenization.

Of course, Americanization via globalization is still a very powerful force. One should never underestimate it. But somehow, more than a decade after the fall of the Berlin Wall, it no longer seems inevitable that everyone is going to look, speak, sing, dance, and think like an American because of globalization.

As it happens, "globalization of the local" is an expression I first saw used by an Indian-born expert on globalization and cultural identity, Indrajit Banerjee, the secretary general of the Asian Media Information and Communication Centre (AMIC). In an interview with Felix Soh of *The Straits Times* of Singapore (September 11, 2005), Banerjee explained that he coined the term to describe the phenomenon that allows dias-

[366] to preserve: to keep from decay
[367] frigid: cold
[368] 3M: American multinational conglomerate
[369] to uproot yourself: to leave your place of origin

pora[370] communities around the world to use today's global media networks to cling to[371] their local mores,[372] news, traditions, and friends – no matter where they are living. As Soh put it in the introduction to his interview with Banerjee, globalization of the local "is globalization in reverse. Instead of global media enveloping Asia, the region's 'local' media are going global. This phenomenon of the globalization of the local is being driven by the demand for local news and information from Asia's diasporas, notably the millions of Chinese and Indian émigrés now living in all parts of the world."

Banerjee, who has a Ph.D. in communications from the Sorbonne, in Paris, sees this from his perch in Singapore, where he teaches at a university: "One would think that globalization in Asia would mean going English, but that's not the case," he said in the interview with *The Straits Times*. "The diasporic market means you can have international newspapers, international TV and radio channels which are completely based on local languages. This is what I call the globalization of the local. It is not the global which comes and envelops us. It is the local which goes global."

Today Britain and the United States have television channels where the programming is all in Chinese, Spanish, Arabic, or Japanese. "If you have populations spread all over the world, then you can use effectively the satellite platforms to broadcast to pockets[373] all over the world," added Banerjee. "If you put these pockets together, they become a huge global market."

Soh pointed out that Zee TV, the biggest Indian entertainment network, had blazed a trail[374] for other Indian TV channels to go regional in Asia. Said Banerjee: "Zee TV has a very clear Indian market – it is the Indian diaspora. Its programming is in Hindi. For Zee TV, competition is really not an issue. It doesn't want to capture the other language audiences." He added, "Also, in the near future, Asia will be a major producer of media content, which is a very positive development. For a long time, Asia was a receiver of content from the West. Now because we're coming of age[375] and becoming mature, our media experiences are

---

[370] diaspora: the movement of people from any nation or group away from their own country

[371] to cling to: to hold tightly to s.th.

[372] mores ['mɔːreɪz]: customs

[373] pocket: (here): small group

[374] to blaze a trail (fig.): to be the first to do s.th. that others follow

[375] to come of age: to develop

substantial. This, together with the rich culture and heritage[376] of Asia, presents the region with tremendous potential to be a content-trading hub.[377] India has one of the world's biggest film industries. It is producing a lot of television content. South Korea and Japan are very strong in animation ... My belief is that the global is going to be interesting only if it is a range[378] of the local. The whole diversity of local experiences and local content is present, rather than one content producer, one language, one cultural perspective and one ideology dominating the world."

India, for instance, has exploded[379] recently as a platform for the outsourcing of game designs and cartoon animation. I was struck by[380] something the head of one of these companies said to me when I visited. Ashish Kulkarni, COO[381] of JadooWorks in Bangalore, explained that India had an abundance of traditional artists, who were able to make the transition easily to computerized digital painting. Many of these artists are the children of Hindu temple sculptors and painters. "We train them to transform their traditional skills to animation in a digital format," said Kulkarni. But to keep up their traditional Indian painting skills, JadooWorks also had set aside a room where artists could retreat[382] to indulge in[383] their native artistry – because the two skills reinforce[384] each other. Companies like JadooWorks come and go with the demands of the global market and who can offer the best, cheapest artists at any given time. But before the world got flat, India had virtually no companies doing this business at all. Now, a new generation of Indian artists at least has a chance to maintain or advance their skills rather than drive taxis to earn a living. "We now tell the parents: 'If your kids are doing well in drawing in seventh grade, you must think of making a career in animation,'" said Kulkarni. "That was difficult five years back, but today, because of more exposure,[385] we can get people to think they can transform their skills that their fathers had" and thereby hold on to them. I interviewed Deepak Ganguly, a slender twenty-eight-year-old

---

[376] heritage: traditions
[377] hub: center
[378] range: variety
[379] to explode: to expanded rapidly
[380] to be struck by: to be impressed by
[381] COO: Chief Operating Officer, a high-ranking administrator responsible for the daily running of a company
[382] to retreat: to draw back
[383] to indulge in: to spend time doing s.th. you like to do
[384] to reinforce: to strengthen
[385] exposure: publicity

computer artist who was then working at JadooWorks. "My parents are artists, my mother is a sculptor at home," he explained. "My father was a carpet designer, he made designs for Indian carpets. I had a knack[386] for drawing, because I was brought up in this kind of climate, so I came into this field. When I started this animation career, at the time 3-D [computers for drawing] were not here in India ... So I did a course in 2-D classical animation and I was a 2-D animator. When this 3-D boom happened in India [in the past couple years], I decided to jump. I was working at a small studio in Delhi. We used to watch movies and *Star Wars* and their computer-generated things. Then I got the chance to learn that skill." Globalization, said Ganguly, was enabling him to take his skills and now sell them all over the world. "With all the easy sharing in the electronic media," he said, "we can get the work here easier, we can send our skills over there easier."

To listen to some of the critics, though, you would think that globalization was only about the spread of crass[387] capitalism, global brands, fast food, and consumer values all crowding out warm, cozy, thriving local communities, industries, and cultures. There is no question that the forces of globalization do some or all of these things in many places on many days. But globalization is not simply about the spread of capitalism or markets or enhanced[388] trade. It is not an exclusively economic phenomenon and its impact is not exclusively economic. It is a much broader, deeper, and more complex phenomenon, involving new forms of communication and innovation. The flattening of the world is about the creation of a global platform for multiple forms of sharing work, knowledge, and entertainment. Worrying about the pulverizing[389] effects of globalization is very legitimate, indeed very important, but ignoring its ability also to empower individuals and enrich our cultural cornucopia[390] misses its potentially positive effects on human freedom and diversity. My point here is not that the flattening of the world will always enrich and preserve culture. My point is that it doesn't always destroy culture, which is the message you hear if you listen only to the globalization critics. The iron law of globalization is very simple: If you think it is all good or all bad, you don't get it. Globalization has empowering and disempowering, homogenizing and particularizing, democra-

[386] knack [næk]: talent
[387] crass: purely materialistic
[388] enhanced: increased
[389] to pulverize (fig.): to destroy s.th. completely
[390] cornucopia [ˌkɔ:nju'kəʊpiə]: abundance

disempower – entmachten
homogenizing –
particularize –

tizing and authoritarian tendencies all built into it. It is about the global market, but it is also about the Internet and Google.

One should have no doubt – I certainly don't – that the flat world empowers the forces of darkness as well as the forces of light. You can upload homemade pornography, homegrown racism, lies, conspiracy theories, and just plain hokum,[391] and spread them easier, faster, and farther on the flat-world platform as well. *The New York Times,* on December 19, 2005, ran a chilling[392] front page story about a teenage boy, Justin Berry, "who was drawn into performing in front of [a] Webcam – undressing, showering, masturbating and even having sex – for an audience of more than 1,500 people, who paid him, over the years, hundreds of thousands of dollars." What is really ironic is that they often paid him by using PayPal.com – the online payment system owned by eBay to make it easy for individuals to buy and sell on its auction site.

For all these reasons, our job is not to trash[393] this platform but to get the best out of it and to prevent the worst.

The kind of globalization we are talking about now – with the Internet and the flattening of the world – "is a different kind of globalization than the one that is in the minds of the people who have been criticizing globalization," remarked Israeli political theorist Yaron Ezrahi. "It has different opportunities and dangers." In cultural terms, the globalization of the local "is allowing a local group of human rights supporters to become part of an international community and feel that solidarity, and the same with environmentalists. And the same, unfortunately, is true with neo-Nazis and al-Qaeda sympathizers. Wherever human beings have the freedom to create communities, they can create progressive or criminal ones ... But the fact is that the Internet has magnified[394] the capacity of individuals to generate their own stories and inscribe themselves[395] on the world, both as individuals and as part of communities. Should we be against that? Of course not."

As of the printing of this book, Google was available in 116 different languages, from Arabic to Zulu to several versions of Chinese. The more people can easily inform themselves in their own languages, the more likely those languages and texts are to survive and the more likely

---

[391] hokum ['həʊkəm]: nonsense
[392] chilling: frightening
[393] to trash: (here): to sharply criticize
[394] to magnify: to make bigger
[395] inscribe themselves: (here): make their presence felt

others will write in them and not feel compelled[396] to switch to English. Search is one of the ten flatteners, and the globalization of the local will be steadily enhanced as search engines gradually spread to every corner of the flat world.

But the flattening of the world is bringing diversity to different corners of the world, even without the Internet. There is more radio today, more TV, more phone, more travel, more trade. The Ghana-born Princeton professor and philosopher Kwame Anthony Appiah expressed this well in an essay for *The New York Times Magazine* (January 1, 2006) titled "The Case for Contamination." Using a visit to his mother in Kumasi, Ghana – the town he grew up in – he adduced[397] a variety of examples to make the point that people in Africa today, even villagers, are not just objects that the West or the modern world inscribes itself upon. They are also subjects – subjects who are in a much more dynamic give-and-take-adopt, adapt, import, re-export, and innovate-relationship with the world, thanks to globalization. "Yes, globalization can produce homogeneity," he wrote. "But globalization is also a threat to homogeneity ... When people talk of the homogeneity produced by globalization, what they are talking about is this: Even here, the villagers will have radios (though the language will be local); you will be able to get a discussion going about Ronaldo, Mike Tyson, or Tupac; and you will probably be able to find a bottle of Guinness or Coca-Cola (as well as of Star or Club, Ghana's own fine lagers). But has access to these things made the place more homogeneous or less? And what can you tell about people's souls from the fact that they drink Coca-Cola? It's true that the enclaves of homogeneity you find these days – in Asante as in Pennsylvania – are less distinctive than they were a century ago, but mostly in good ways. More of them have access to effective medicines. More of them have access to clean drinking water, and more of them have schools. Where, as is still too common, they don't have these things, it's something not to celebrate but to deplore.[398] And whatever loss of difference there has been, they are constantly inventing new forms of difference: new hairstyles, new slang, even, from time to time, new religions. No one could say that the world's villages are becoming anything like the same."

The newest anti-homogenizing force is podcasting – a whole new tool for globalizing the local. I got a glimpse into this phenomenon in October 2005 when I visited a small apartment in suburban Shanghai

[396] to compel: to force
[397] to adduce: to offer as proof
[398] to deplore: to strongly disapprove of s.th.

that is home to China's leading podcasting Web site, Toodou.com. "We already have thirteen thousand channels on our site, and about five thousand of them are updated regularly," explained Gary Wang, thirty-two, the Fuzhou-born and U.S.- and French-educated Chinese engineer who founded Toodou, which means "potato" in Chinese. Any Chinese can create his or her own channel of video or audio content on Toodou, and other individuals sign up to get the content on that channel each time new material is uploaded. For now, the service is free; eventually Toodou will charge a monthly subscription.

"I want to create hundreds of thousands of different channels, maintained by just average people, where other people can access them and download the material," added Wang. And he will, because the ease of uploading and podcasting means there are almost no barriers to entry, as long as you have a computer, a camera, and a microphone. (There are still political limits on what you can say from China, but who knows how long those limits will be sustainable.[399] Toodou.com censors porn and anything that violates Chinese law or directly threatens the Communist government.)

Toodou's most popular podcast when I visited was a video of two twenty-year-old Chinese women lip-synching a popular Cantonese rock tune. "They got bored,"[400] explained Wang, so they went out and bought their own Webcam (which can be found in Shanghai for the equivalent of $6), used Microsoft Movie Maker (software that comes bundled with Windows XP), made their own three-minute MTV-like podcast, and uploaded it onto Toodou.com. It was viewed seventy-five thousand times in the first three months. "It took them one hour to make and fifteen minutes to edit," said Wang. The girls, who call themselves "The Beans," now have their own online fan club.

Another favorite is a podcast by two Chinese architecture students wearing Houston Rockets jerseys[401] (the team of Chinese-born NBA[402] star Yao Ming) and lip-synching a Backstreet Boys tune. A slide show[403] on life in Shenzhen had been viewed sixteen thousand times, prompting all sorts of accompanying commentary from viewers around China. The second-highest-viewed podcast when I visited was a concert by an underground rock band at a Shanghai bar. Toodou's goal, said Wang,

---

[399] sustainable: able to continue in the same way
[400] bored: restless due to a lack of interest
[401] jersey ['dʒɜːzi]: shirt that is worn by players in a sports game
[402] NBA: National Football Association
[403] slide show: a continually changing series of photographs

"will be to connect [Chinese] people to their tastes and to their potential collaborators. We will have a huge content database and we will share the revenue[404] with content providers." Wang added: "We created this platform for free participation, and people [just] come in. With all kinds of tools becoming cheaper and cheaper, the creative part of people will naturally grow."

Yes, I know, I am a little ahead of myself. Very few Chinese have ever even seen an iPod, so most of the podcasting that does exist here is created and viewed or heard on PCs. Once the price of an iPod (music or video) comes down, though, there will be a huge podcast market here. Many of the current podcasts are junk,[405] but the quality, too, will surely improve. The ease of podcasting will force competition and experimentation. Wang first heard of podcasting only in 2004. Some thirteen months later he had the most popular podcasting site in China, with one hundred thousand registered users, eight employees, forty volunteers, and a U.S. venture capital backer. News of his site was spread for free by Chinese bloggers. The office/apartment he was using when I visited rents for $500 a month, and some of his employees also slept there. Almost all the software that runs Toodou.com is from free, open-source material on the Web – an Apache Webserver; FreeBSD, a free Unix operating system; MySQL, a free database system; and PHP, free programming language. Wang wrote the algorithms that run Toodou.com himself. Comparing China to America and Europe, where he studied, Wang said, "With the same amount of money, I can do ten times more here ... I can live on $1,000 a month in Shanghai and have the latest technology and all these servers – anything you can find in the U.S. is here."

In China, the combination of low costs and lowered barriers is making the process of creating cultural content cheaper and as a result more popular. That's why I am confident that this flattening phase of globalization is not going to mean more Americanization, but more globalization of local cultures, art forms, styles, recipes, literature, videos, and opinions – more and more local content made global.

"We have different songs [than Americans] and we want to express different things, but the desire is the same," said Wang. "We all want to be seen and heard and be able to create stuff we like and share it ... People from all over the world will draw knowledge and inspiration from the same technology platform, but different cultures will flourish on it. It is the same soil, but different trees will grow."

---

[404] revenue: money earned
[405] junk: poor quality

And you thought the Cultural Revolution was over. Sorry, it's just beginning. Only China's newest Cultural Revolution is going to be driven this time from the bottom up – thanks to the flat-world platform – by podcasters with Apple's little white iPods, not from the top down by Maoists[406] with Little Red Books.[407]

The globalization of the local is not only happening culturally but also commercially. Just as the flattening of the world is starting to equalize and diversify the flow of culture, it is also starting to equalize and diversify the flow of investment – so globalization is no longer driven primarily by American or Western multinationals. More and more Chinese, Indian, Brazilian, Russian, Asian, and even African companies are doing business globally.

The Davos World Economic Forum is always a useful barometer of global trends, and at Davos 2007, for the first time, I began to really feel the globalization of the local happening in business to a significant degree. First, I had breakfast with Mohammed Shafik Gabr, a leading Egyptian entrepreneur. Shafik's company, the Artoc Group for Investment and Development, was involved in building two new cities in Egypt from the ground up, but that's not what struck me most. I was struck by the managers Shafik was recruiting to Cairo to run his rapidly expanding company. He explained to me that he had just hired as his new group COO an American of Egyptian origin who had worked for Coca-Cola in Atlanta, London, and Africa; he had hired an American Asia expert based in Hong Kong as his vice chairman for policy and business development; and he had hired a Frenchman as group general manager for his real estate subsidiary. It was clear that Shafik was preparing to go aggressively into new markets – the "new markets" of America, Asia, and France! A week later (January 31, 2007), the *Financial Times* carried the following lead story: "Tata Steel of India won the battle to control Anglo-Dutch steelmaker Corus on Wednesday, after more than eight hours of head-to-head bidding[408] against Companhia Siderurgica Nacional of Brazil." This was the first large foreign acquisition by an Indian company, and it was a doozy[409] – £6.2 billion to take over

[406] Maoists: followers of Mao Zedong, the first chairman of the Communist Party of China

[407] Little Red Book: a famous book of sayings from Mao that was published with a red cover

[408] to bid: to offer ever higher sums of money for s.th.

[409] doozy (colloquial): an extraordinary example of s.th.

Corus, which owns almost the entire steel industries of Britain and the Netherlands. So an Indian company outbid a Brazilian company to take over the biggest steel companies in Britain and the Netherlands!

In the middle of the Davos forum, Nathan Gardels, editor *of Global Viewpoint* magazine, wrote an essay for the *International Herald Tribune* (January 24, 2007) that summarized these trends: "Globalization now belongs to everyone who can figure out how to take advantage of its opportunities and minimize its dislocations. American-bred technology may be its midwife,[410] but Americans are no longer solely the parents. That's a big power shift indeed."

Indeed, if these trends continue, it is inevitable that globalization will finally become, well, *global* –both culturally and commercially – a process no longer driven from America and Europe but from all four corners of the flat world.

[410] midwife: a woman who helps in the delivery of a baby

Fareed Zakaria was born in Mumbai (Bombay), India in 1964. After moving to the United States, he went on to receive a B.A. from Yale College and a Ph.D. from Harvard University. Currently, he is the host of CNN's flagship international affairs program, Fareed Zakaria GPS, which has been broadcast in more than 200 million homes in over 210 countries. In addition, he is Editor at Large of TIME magazine, a Washington Post columnist, and a New York Times bestselling author. He was described in 1999 by Esquire Magazine as "the most influential foreign policy adviser of his generation." In 2010, Foreign Policy magazine named him one of the top 100 global thinkers. He lives in New York City with his wife, and has a son and two daughters.

The article below was later expanded into his book, *The Post-American World*. In this text, Zakaria gives examples of how global power relationships have changed dramatically in recent years, and offers evidence that they will continue to do so in the foreseeable future. He considers these changes to be positive and argues that they represent a shared understanding of the world which is vital to the kind of cooperation necessary to solve global problems. While acknowledging these problems, he also cautions about the effects of media hyperbole[1] by offering a well-needed sense of perspective. You can watch an interview with Fareed Zakaria at: http://www.youtube.com/watch?v=wA7srwym3Yk.

1 hyperbole [haɪˈpɜːbli]: exaggeration, overstatement

The Rise of the Rest[2]

by Fareed Zakaria

It's true China is booming, Russia is growing more assertive, terrorism is a threat. But if America is losing the ability to dictate to this new world, it has not lost the ability to lead.

Americans are glum[3] at the moment. No, I mean really glum. In April, a new poll[4] revealed that 81 percent of the American people believe that the country is on the "wrong track." In the 25 years that pollsters have asked this question, last month's response was by far the most negative. Other polls, asking similar questions, found levels of gloom[5] that were even more alarming, often at 30- and 40-year highs. There are reasons to be pessimistic – a financial panic and looming[6] recession, a seemingly endless war in Iraq, and the ongoing threat of terrorism. But the facts on the ground – unemployment numbers, foreclosure rates,[7] deaths from terror attacks – are simply not dire[8] enough to explain the present atmosphere of malaise.

American anxiety springs[9] from something much deeper, a sense that large and disruptive forces are coursing[10] through the world. In almost every industry, in every aspect of life, it feels like the patterns of the past are being scrambled.[11] "Whirl[12] is king, having driven out Zeus,"[13] wrote Aristophanes 2,400 years ago. And – for the first time in living memory – the United States does not seem to be leading the charge.[14] Americans

---

[2] Fareed Zakaria, *The Rise of the Rest*, *Newsweek*, May 03, 2008.
[3] glum: depressed
[4] poll: the result of questions asked to determine people's opinion on an issue
[5] gloom: depressive atmosphere
[6] to loom: (here): to be about to happen
[7] foreclosure rates: percent of properties taken back by banks due to the inability of borrowers to repay their loans
[8] dire: threatening
[9] to spring: to arise
[10] to course: to flow
[11] to scramble: to mix up
[12] whirl [wɜ:l] (fig.): rapid change
[13] Zeus [zju:s]: King of the gods in Greek mythology
[14] charge: rush forward

see that a new world is coming into being, but fear it is one being shaped in distant lands and by foreign people.

Look around. The world's tallest building is in Taipei, and will soon be in Dubai. Its largest publicly traded company is in Beijing. Its biggest refinery is being constructed in India. Its largest passenger airplane is built in Europe. The largest investment fund on the planet is in Abu Dhabi; the biggest movie industry is Bollywood, not Hollywood. Once quintessentially[15] American icons have been usurped[16] by the natives. The largest Ferris wheel is in Singapore. The largest casino is in Macao, which overtook Las Vegas in gambling revenues[17] last year. America no longer dominates even its favorite sport, shopping. The Mall of America in Minnesota once boasted[18] that it was the largest shopping mall in the world. Today it wouldn't make the top ten. In the most recent rankings, only two of the world's ten richest people are American. These lists are arbitrary and a bit silly, but consider that only ten years ago, the United States would have serenely[19] topped almost every one of these categories.

These factoids reflect a seismic shift[20] in power and attitudes. It is one that I sense when I travel around the world. In America, we are still debating the nature and extent of anti-Americanism. One side says that the problem is real and worrying and that we must woo[21] the world back. The other says this is the inevitable price of power and that many of these countries are envious – and vaguely French – so we can safely ignore their griping.[22] But while we argue over why they hate us, "they" have moved on, and are now far more interested in other, more dynamic parts of the globe. The world has shifted from anti-Americanism to post-Americanism.

I. The End of Pax Americana

During the 1980s, when I would visit India – where I grew up – most Indians were fascinated by the United States. Their interest, I have to confess, was not in the important power players in Washington or the

[15] quintessentially: typically
[16] to usurp [juˈzɜːp]: to take over
[17] revenues (plural) [ˈrevənjuːz]: money earned
[18] to boast: to say proudly
[19] serenely: calmly
[20] seismic shift (fig.): dramatic change
[21] to woo [wuː]: to try win the affection of s.o.
[22] to gripe (colloquial): to complain

great intellectuals in Cambridge.[23] People would often ask me about ... Donald Trump. He was the very symbol of the United States – brassy,[24] rich, and modern. He symbolized the feeling that if you wanted to find the biggest and largest anything, you had to look to America. Today, outside of entertainment figures, there is no comparable interest in American personalities. If you wonder why, read India's newspapers or watch its television. There are dozens of Indian businessmen who are now wealthier than the Donald. Indians are obsessed[25] by their own vulgar real estate billionaires. And that newfound interest in their own story is being replicated across much of the world.

How much? Well, consider this fact. In 2006 and 2007, 124 countries grew their economies at over 4 percent a year. That includes more than 30 countries in Africa. Over the last two decades, lands outside the industrialized West have been growing at rates that were once unthinkable. While there have been booms and busts, the overall trend has been unambiguously[26] upward. Antoine van Agtmael, the fund manager who coined the term "emerging markets," has identified the 25 companies most likely to be the world's next great multinationals. His list includes four companies each from Brazil, Mexico, South Korea, and Taiwan; three from India, two from China, and one each from Argentina, Chile, Malaysia, and South Africa. This is something much broader than the much-ballyhooed[27] rise of China or even Asia. It is the rise of the rest – the rest of the world.

We are living through the third great power shift in modern history. The first was the rise of the Western world, around the 15th century. It produced the world as we know it now – science and technology, commerce and capitalism, the industrial and agricultural revolutions. It also led to the prolonged political dominance of the nations of the Western world. The second shift, which took place in the closing years of the 19th century, was the rise of the United States. Once it industrialized, it soon became the most powerful nation in the world, stronger than any likely combination of other nations. For the last 20 years, America's superpower status in every realm[28] has been largely unchallenged –some-

---

[23] Cambridge ['keɪmbrɪdʒ]: town near Boston, Massachusetts where Harvard University and MIT are located

[24] brassy (colloquial): shamelessly bold

[25] obsessed: constantly worried about s.th.

[26] unambiguously: clearly

[27] ballyhooed [ˌbæli'hu:d]: exaggerated

[28] realm: area

thing that's never happened before in history, at least since the Roman Empire dominated the known world 2,000 years ago. During this Pax Americana, the global economy has accelerated dramatically. And that expansion is the driver behind the third great power shift of the modern age – the rise of the rest.

At the military and political level, we still live in a unipolar world. But along every other dimension –industrial, financial, social, cultural – the distribution of power is shifting, moving away from American dominance. In terms of war and peace, economics and business, ideas and art, this will produce a landscape that is quite different from the one we have lived in until now – one defined and directed from many places and by many peoples.

The strongest argument favoring a globalized economy ...

The post-American world is naturally an unsettling prospect for Americans, but it should not be. This will not be a world defined by the decline of America but rather the rise of everyone else. It is the result of a series of positive trends that have been progressing over the last 20 years, trends that have created an international climate of unprecedented[29] peace and prosperity.

[29] unprecedented: for the first time

I know. That's not the world that people perceive.[30] We are told that we live in dark, dangerous times. Terrorism, rogue states,[31] nuclear proliferation,[32] financial panics, recession, outsourcing, and illegal immigrants all loom large[33] in the national discourse. Al Qaeda, Iran, North Korea, China, Russia are all threats in some way or another. But just how violent is today's world, really?

A team of scholars at the University of Maryland has been tracking deaths caused by organized violence. Their data show that wars of all kinds have been declining since the mid-1980s and that we are now at the lowest levels of global violence since the 1950s. Deaths from terrorism are reported to have risen in recent years. But on closer examination, 80 percent of those casualties[34] come from Afghanistan and Iraq, which are really war zones with ongoing insurgencies[35] – and the overall numbers remain small. Looking at the evidence, Harvard's polymath[36] professor Steven Pinker has ventured to speculate that we are probably living "in the most peaceful time of our species' existence."

Why does it not feel that way? Why do we think we live in scary times? Part of the problem is that as violence has been ebbing,[37] information has been exploding. The last 20 years have produced an information revolution that brings us news and, most crucially, images from around the world all the time. The immediacy of the images and the intensity of the 24-hour news cycle combine to produce constant hype. Every weather disturbance is the "storm of the decade." Every bomb that explodes is BREAKING NEWS. Because the information revolution is so new, we – reporters, writers, readers, viewers – are all just now figuring out how to put everything in context.

We didn't watch daily footage of the two million people who died in Indochina in the 1970s, or the million who perished in the sands of the Iran-Iraq war ten years later. We saw little of the civil war in the Congo in the 1990s, where millions died. But today any bomb that goes off, any

---

[30] to perceive: to be aware of
[31] rogue [rəʊg] state: a state that acts illegally or causes international troubles
[32] proliferation: sudden increase in the amount of s.th.
[33] loom large: (here): repeatedly appear as topics
[34] casualty: a person who has died
[35] insurgency: revolt, rebellion against the government
[36] polymath: being an expert in many different fields
[37] to ebb (fig.): to become gradually less

rocket that is fired, any death that results, is documented by someone, somewhere and ricochets[38] instantly across the world. Add to this terrorist attacks, which are random[39] and brutal. "That could have been me," you think. Actually, your chances of being killed in a terrorist attack are tiny – for an American, smaller than drowning in your bathtub. But it doesn't feel like that.

The threats we face are real. Islamic jihadists are a nasty bunch – they do want to attack civilians everywhere. But it is increasingly clear that militants and suicide bombers make up a tiny portion of the world's 1.3 billion Muslims. They can do real damage, especially if they get their hands on nuclear weapons. But the combined efforts of the world's governments have effectively put them on the run and continue to track them and their money. Jihad persists,[40] but the jihadists have had to scatter, work in small local cells, and use simple and undetectable weapons. They have not been able to hit big, symbolic targets, especially ones involving Americans. So they blow up bombs in cafés, marketplaces, and subway stations. The problem is that in doing so, they kill locals and alienate ordinary Muslims. Look at the polls. Support for violence of any kind has dropped dramatically over the last five years in all Muslim countries.

Militant groups have reconstituted in certain areas where they exploit a particular local issue or have support from a local ethnic group or sect, most worryingly in Pakistan and Afghanistan where Islamic radicalism has become associated with Pashtun[41] identity politics. But as a result, these groups are becoming more local and less global. Al Qaeda in Iraq, for example, has turned into a group that is more anti-Shiite than anti-American. The bottom line[42] is this: since 9/11, Al Qaeda Central, the gang run by Osama bin Laden, has not been able to launch a single major terror attack in the West or any Arab country – its original targets. They used to do terrorism, now they make videotapes. Of course one day they will get lucky again, but that they have been stymied[43] for almost seven years points out that in this battle between governments and terror groups, the former need not despair.

---

[38] to ricochet ['rɪkəʃeɪ]: to bounce off
[39] random: without any pattern
[40] to persist: to continue
[41] Pashtun: having to do with an ethnic group living both in Afghanistan and Pakistan
[42] bottom line: the result
[43] to stymie ['staɪmi]: to block

Some point to the dangers posed by countries like Iran. These rogue states present real problems, but look at them in context. The American economy is 68 times the size of Iran's. Its military budget is 110 times that of the mullahs. Were Iran to attain a nuclear capacity, it would complicate the geopolitics of the Middle East. But none of the problems we face compare with the dangers posed by a rising Germany in the first half of the 20th century or an expansionist Soviet Union in the second half. Those were great global powers bent on[44] world domination. If this is 1938, as some neoconservatives tell us, then Iran is Romania, not Germany.

Others paint a dark picture of a world in which dictators are on the march. China and Russia and assorted other oil potentates[45] are surging.[46] We must draw the battle lines now, they warn, and engage in a great Manichean struggle[47] that will define the next century. Some of John McCain's[48] rhetoric has suggested that he adheres to[49] this dire, dyspeptic[50] view. But before we all sign on for a new Cold War, let's take a deep breath and gain some perspective. Today's rising great powers are relatively benign[51] by historical measure. In the past, when countries grew rich they've wanted to become great military powers, overturn the existing order, and create their own empires or spheres of influence. But since the rise of Japan and Germany in the 1960s and 1970s, none have done this, choosing instead to get rich within the existing international order. China and India are clearly moving in this direction. Even Russia, the most aggressive and revanchist great power today, has done little that compares with past aggressors. The fact that for the first time in history, the United States can contest Russian influence in Ukraine – a country 4,800 miles away from Washington that Russia has dominated or ruled for 350 years – tells us something about the balance of power between the West and Russia.

Compare Russia and China with where they were 35 years ago. At the time both (particularly Russia) were great power threats, actively conspiring against the United States, arming guerrilla movement across the

---

[44] to be bent on: to be determined
[45] potentate: power, dominant country
[46] to surge: to grow rapidly
[47] Manichean [ˌmænɪˈkiːən] struggle: a battle between good and bad
[48] John McCain (1936–): Republican senator and unsuccessful presidential candidate
[49] to adhere to (formal): to stick firmly to s.th.
[50] dyspeptic [dɪsˈpeptɪk] (formal): disagreeable, irritable
[51] benign [bəˈnaɪn]: not dangerous

globe, funding insurgencies and civil wars, blocking every American plan in the United Nations. Now they are more integrated into the global economy and society than at any point in at least 100 years. They occupy an uncomfortable gray zone, neither friends nor foes, cooperating with the United States and the West on some issues, obstructing[52] others. But how large is their potential for trouble? Russia's military spending is $35 billion, or 1/20th of the Pentagon's. China has about 20 nuclear missiles that can reach the United States. We have 830 missiles, most with multiple warheads, that can reach China. Who should be worried about whom? Other rising autocracies like Saudi Arabia and the Gulf states are close U.S. allies that shelter[53] under America's military protection, buy its weapons, invest in its companies, and follow many of its diktats.[54] With Iran's ambitions growing in the region, these countries are likely to become even closer allies, unless America gratuitously[55] alienates them.

II. The Good News

In July 2006, I spoke with a senior member of the Israeli government, a few days after Israel's war with Hezbollah had ended. He was genuinely worried about his country's physical security. Hezbollah's rockets had reached farther into Israel than people had believed possible. The military response had clearly been ineffectual: Hezbollah launched as many rockets on the last day of the war as on the first. Then I asked him about the economy – the area in which he worked. His response was striking. "That's puzzled all of us," he said. "The stock market was higher on the last day of the war than on the first! The same with the shekel."[56] The government was spooked,[57] but the market wasn't.

Or consider the Iraq War, which has produced deep, lasting chaos and dysfunction in that country. Over two million refugees[58] have crowded into neighboring[59] lands. That would seem to be the kind of political crisis guaranteed to spill over. But as I've traveled in the Middle East over the last few years, I've been struck by how little Iraq's troubles have destabi-

---

[52] to obstruct: to block
[53] to shelter: to take cover
[54] diktat: order that must be obeyed
[55] gratuitously: needlessly
[56] shekel: Israeli currency
[57] to spook (colloquial): to scare
[58] refugee: person in exile
[59] neighboring: bordering

lized the region. Everywhere you go, people angrily denounce American foreign policy. But most Middle Eastern countries are booming. Iraq's neighbors – Turkey, Jordan, and Saudi Arabia – are enjoying unprecedented prosperity. The Gulf states are busy modernizing their economies and societies, asking the Louvre, New York University, and Cornell Medical School to set up remote branches in the desert. There's little evidence of chaos, instability, and rampant[60] Islamic fundamentalism.

The underlying reality across the globe is of enormous vitality. For the first time ever, most countries around the world are practicing sensible economics. Consider inflation. Over the past 20 years hyperinflation, a problem that used to bedevil[61] large swaths[62] of the world from Turkey to Brazil to Indonesia, has largely vanished,[63] tamed[64] by successful fiscal and monetary policies. The results are clear and stunning. The share of people living on $1 a day has plummeted[65] from 40 percent in 1981 to 18 percent in 2004 and is estimated to drop to 12 percent by 2015. Poverty is falling in countries that house 80 percent of the world's population. There remains real poverty in the world – most worryingly in 50 basket-case[66] countries that contain 1 billion people – but the overall trend has never been more encouraging. The global economy has more than doubled in size over the last 15 years and is now approaching $54 trillion! Global trade has grown by 133 percent in the same period. The expansion of the global economic pie[67] has been so large, with so many countries participating, that it has become the dominating force of the current[68] era. Wars, terrorism, and civil strife[69] cause disruptions temporarily[70] but eventually they are overwhelmed by the waves of globalization. These circumstances[71] may not last, but it is worth understanding what the world has looked like for the past few decades.

---

[60] rampant: spreading uncontrollably
[61] to bedevil: to trouble
[62] swath: area
[63] to vanish: to disappear
[64] to tame: to control
[65] to plummet: to drop dramatically
[66] basket-case (fig.): poorly functioning
[67] pie: (here): total of what there is to divide up
[68] current: present
[69] strife: conflict
[70] temporarily: for a short time
[71] circumstances: conditions

III. A New Nationalism

Of course, global growth is also responsible for some of the biggest problems in the world right now. It has produced tons of money – what businesspeople call liquidity – that moves around the world. The combination of low inflation and lots of cash has meant low interest rates, which in turn have made people act greedily[72] and/or stupidly. So we have witnessed over the last two decades a series of bubbles – in East Asian countries, technology stocks, housing, subprime mortgages,[73] and emerging market equities.[74] Growth also explains one of the signature[75] events of our times – soaring commodity prices.[76] $100 oil is just the tip of the barrel.[77] Almost all commodities are at 200-year highs. Food, only a few decades ago in danger of price collapse, is now in the midst[78] of a scary rise. None of this is due to[79] dramatic fall-offs in supply. It is demand, growing global demand, that is fueling these prices. The effect of more and more people eating, drinking, washing, driving, and consuming will have seismic effects on the global system. These may be high-quality problems, but they are deep problems nonetheless.

The most immediate effect of global growth is the appearance of new economic powerhouses on the scene. It is an accident of history that for the last several centuries, the richest countries in the world have all been very small in terms of[80] population. Denmark has 5.5 million people, the Netherlands has 16.6 million. The United States is the biggest of the bunch and has dominated the advanced industrial world. But the real giants – China, India, Brazil – have been sleeping, unable or unwilling to join the world of functioning economies. Now they are on the move and naturally, given their size, they will have a large footprint on the map of the future. Even if people in these countries remain relatively poor, as nations their total wealth will be massive. Or to put it another way, any number, no matter how small, when multiplied by 2.5 billion

72 greedily: *gierig*
73 subprime mortgage: mortgage (*Hypothek*) given to s.o. who may be unable to repay the loan
74 equities (plural): the total value of all the stocks of a company
75 signature: (here): defining
76 soaring commodity prices: the high rise in the price of goods
77 tip of the barrel: (here): just the beginning
78 midst: middle
79 due to: caused by
80 in terms of: based on

becomes a very big number. (2.5 billion is the population of China plus India.)

The rise of China and India is really just the most obvious manifestation of a rising world. In dozens of big countries, one can see the same set of forces at work – a growing economy, a resurgent[81] society, a vibrant culture, and a rising sense of national pride. That pride can morph into[82] something uglier. For me, this was vividly[83] illustrated a few years ago when I was chatting with a young Chinese executive in an Internet café in Shanghai. He wore Western clothes, spoke fluent English, and was immersed[84] in global pop culture. He was a product of globalization and spoke its language of bridge building and cosmopolitan values. At least, he did so until we began talking about Taiwan, Japan, and even the United States. (We did not discuss Tibet, but I'm sure had we done so, I could have added it to this list.) His responses were filled with passion, bellicosity,[85] and intolerance. I felt as if I were in Germany in 1910, speaking to a young German professional, who would have been equally modern and yet also a staunch nationalist.

As economic fortunes rise, so inevitably[86] does nationalism. Imagine that your country has been poor and marginal[87] for centuries. Finally, things turn around and it becomes a symbol of economic progress and success. You would be proud, and anxious that your people win recognition and respect throughout the world.

In many countries such nationalism arises from a pent-up[88] frustration over having to accept an entirely Western, or American, narrative[89] of world history – one in which they are miscast[90] or remain bit players.[91] Russians have long chafed[92] over the manner in which Western countries

[81] resurgent: returning to life
[82] to morph into: to transform into s.th.
[83] vividly: clearly
[84] to immerse: to go deep into s.th.
[85] bellicosity: aggression
[86] inevitably: unavoidably
[87] marginal: unimportant
[88] pent-up: built up
[89] narrative: story
[90] to miscast: to give an actor or actress a role that does not fit him or her
[91] bit player: actor or actress with a small part
[92] to chafe: to be irritated by s.th.

remember World War II. The American narrative is one in which the United States and Britain heroically defeat the forces of fascism. The Normandy landings are the climactic highpoint of the war – the beginning of the end. The Russians point out, however, that in fact the entire Western front was a sideshow.[93] Three quarters of all German forces were engaged on the Eastern front fighting Russian troops, and Germany suffered 70 percent of its casualties there. The Eastern front involved more land combat than all other theaters[94] of World War II put together.

Such divergent[95] national perspectives always existed. But today, thanks to the information revolution, they are amplified,[96] echoed, and disseminated. Where once there were only the narratives laid out[97] by *The New York Times*, *Time*, *Newsweek*, the BBC, and CNN, there are now dozens of indigenous[98] networks and channels – from Al Jazeera to New Delhi's NDTV to Latin America's Telesur. The result is that the "rest" are now dissecting[99] the assumptions and narratives of the West and providing alternative views. A young Chinese diplomat told me in 2006, "When you tell us that we support a dictatorship in Sudan to have access to its oil, what I want to say is, 'And how is that different from your support of a medieval monarchy in Saudi Arabia?' We see the hypocrisy, we just don't say anything – yet."

The fact that newly rising nations are more strongly asserting[100] their ideas and interests is inevitable in a post-American world. This raises a conundrum[101] – how to get a world of many actors to work together. The traditional mechanisms of international cooperation are fraying.[102] The U.N. Security Council has as its permanent members the victors[103] of a war that ended more than 60 years ago. The G8[104] does not include China, India or Brazil – the three fastest-growing large economies in the

[93] sideshow: not the most import event
[94] theatre: (here): combat zone
[95] divergent: opposing
[96] to amplify: to make more noticeable
[97] to lay out: to present
[98] indigenous: native to a region
[99] to dissect: to take apart
[100] to assert: to state firmly and clearly
[101] conundrum: complex situation that has no simple solution
[102] to fray: to come apart
[103] victor: winner
[104] G8: Group of 8; forum for the eight most economically powerful nations of the world

world – and yet claims to represent the movers and shakers[105] of the world economy. By tradition, the IMF[106] is always headed by a European and the World Bank by an American. This "tradition," like the segregated customs[107] of an old country club, might be charming[108] to an insider. But to the majority who live outside the West, it seems bigoted.[109] Our challenge is this: Whether the problem is a trade dispute[110] or a human rights tragedy like Darfur[111] or climate change, the only solutions that will work are those involving many nations. But arriving at solutions when more countries and more non-governmental players are feeling empowered will be harder than ever.

IV. The Next American Century

Many look at the vitality of this emerging world and conclude that the United States has had its day.[112] "Globalization is striking back," Gabor Steingart, an editor at Germany's leading news magazine, *Der Spiegel*, writes in a best-selling book. As others prosper, he argues, the United States has lost key industries, its people have stopped saving money, and its government has become increasingly indebted to Asian central banks. The current financial crisis has only given greater force to such fears.

But take a step back. Over the last 20 years, globalization has been gaining depth and breadth. America has benefited massively from these trends. It has enjoyed unusually robust growth, low unemployment and inflation, and received hundreds of billions of dollars in investment. These are not signs of economic collapse. Its companies have entered new countries and industries with great success, using global supply chains and technology to stay in the vanguard[113] of efficiency. U.S. exports and manufacturing have actually held their ground and services have boomed.

[105] movers and shakers (colloquial): key players
[106] IMF: International Monetary Fund
[107] segregated customs: practice of barring blacks from membership
[108] charming: very pleasant and attractive
[109] bigoted: prejudiced
[110] dispute: disagreement
[111] Darfur: area in western Sudan that has been the scene of famine and armed conflict
[112] to have one's day (colloquial): to reach a highpoint after which it will never be as good again
[113] vanguard: forefront

The United States is currently ranked as the globe's most competitive economy by the World Economic Forum. It remains dominant in many industries of the future like nanotechnology, biotechnology, and dozens of smaller high-tech fields. Its universities are the finest in the world, making up 8 of the top ten and 37 of the top fifty, according to a prominent ranking produced by Shanghai Jiao Tong University. A few years ago the National Science Foundation put out a scary and much-discussed statistic. In 2004, the group said, 950,000 engineers graduated from China and India, while only 70,000 graduated from the United States. But those numbers are wildly off the mark. If you exclude the car mechanics and repairmen – who are all counted as engineers in Chinese and Indian statistics – the numbers look quite different. Per capita, it turns out, the United States trains more engineers than either of the Asian giants.

But America's hidden secret is that most of these engineers are immigrants. Foreign students and immigrants account for almost 50 percent of all science researchers in the country. In 2006 they received 40 percent of all PhDs. By 2010, 75 percent of all science PhDs in this country will be awarded to foreign students. When these graduates settle in the country, they create economic opportunity. Half of all Silicon Valley start-ups have one founder who is an immigrant or first generation American. The potential for a new burst of American productivity depends not on our education system or R&D[114] spending, but on our immigration policies. If these people are allowed and encouraged to stay, then innovation will happen here. If they leave, they'll take it with them.

More broadly, this is America's great – and potentially insurmountable[115] – strength. It remains the most open, flexible society in the world, able to absorb other people, cultures, ideas, goods, and services. The country thrives on the hunger and energy of poor immigrants. Faced with the new technologies of foreign companies, or growing markets overseas, it adapts and adjusts. When you compare this dynamism with the closed and hierarchical nations that were once superpowers, you sense that the United States is different and may not fall into the trap of becoming rich, and fat, and lazy.

American society can adapt to this new world. But can the American government? Washington has gotten used to a world in which all roads

[114] R&D: research and development
[115] insurmountable: unbeatable

led to its doorstep. America has rarely had to worry about benchmarking[116] to the rest of the world – it was always so far ahead. But the natives have gotten good at capitalism and the gap[117] is narrowing. Look at the rise of London. It's now the world's leading financial center – less because of things that the United States did badly than those London did well, like improving regulation and becoming friendlier to foreign capital. Or take the U.S. health care system, which has become a huge liability[118] for American companies. U.S. carmakers now employ more people in Ontario, Canada, than Michigan because in Canada their health care costs are lower. Twenty years ago, the United States had the lowest corporate taxes in the world. Today they are the second-highest. It's not that ours went up. Those of others went down.

American parochialism[119] is particularly evident in foreign policy. Economically, as other countries grow, for the most part the pie expands and everyone wins. But geopolitics is a struggle for influence: as other nations become more active internationally, they will seek greater freedom of action. This necessarily means that America's unimpeded[120] influence will decline. But if the world that's being created has more power centers, nearly all are interested in order, stability and progress. Rather than narrowly obsessing about our own short-term interests and interest groups, our chief priority should be to bring these rising forces into the global system, to integrate them so that they in turn broaden and deepen global economic, political, and cultural ties. If China, India, Russia, Brazil all feel that they have a stake[121] in the existing global order, there will be less danger of war, depression, panics, and breakdowns. There will be lots of problems, crisis, and tensions, but they will occur against a backdrop of systemic stability. This benefits them but also us. It's the ultimate win-win.

To bring others into this world, the United States needs to make its own commitment to the system clear. So far, America has been able to have it both ways. It is the global rule-maker but doesn't always play by the rules. And forget about standards created by others. Only three coun-

[116] to benchmark: to compare against others
[117] gap: distance of separation
[118] liability: disadvantage
[119] parochialism [pəˈrəʊkiəlˌɪzm]: provincialism
[120] unimpeded: without any interference
[121] stake: interest

tries in the world don't use the metric system – Liberia, Myanmar, and the United States. For America to continue to lead the world, we will have to first join it.

Americans – particularly the American government – have not really understood the rise of the rest. This is one of the most thrilling stories in history. Billions of people are escaping from abject[122] poverty. The world will be enriched and ennobled[123] as they become consumers, producers, inventors, thinkers, dreamers, and doers. This is all happening because of American ideas and actions. For 60 years, the United States has pushed countries to open their markets, free up their politics, and embrace[124] trade and technology. American diplomats, businessmen, and intellectuals have urged people in distant lands to be unafraid of change, to join the advanced world, to learn the secrets of our success. Yet just as they are beginning to do so, we are losing faith in such ideas. We have become suspicious of trade, openness, immigration, and investment because now it's not Americans going abroad but foreigners coming to America. Just as the world is opening up, we are closing down.

Generations from now, when historians write about these times, they might note that by the turn of the 21st century, the United States had succeeded in its great, historical mission – globalizing the world. We don't want them to write that along the way, we forgot to globalize ourselves.

---

[122] abject: extreme
[123] to ennoble: to raise the status
[124] to embrace: (here): to accept with enthusiasm

Muhammad Yunus was born in Chittagong, Bangladesh in 1940. The third of fourteen children, he was educated at Dhaka University and was awarded a Fulbright scholarship to study economics at Vanderbilt University. He then served as chairman of the economics department at Chittagong University before devoting his life to providing financial and social services to the poorest of the poor. He is the founder and managing director of Grameen Bank and the author of the bestselling *Banker to the Poor.* It has been this work of providing small loans to very poor people, and thus allowing them to rise above their circumstances, for which he has become famous. Among numerous awards and honorary degrees, Yunus received the 2006 Nobel Peace Prize. He lives with his wife in Bangladesh and has two daughters.

In the passages which follow, Yunus proposes a new economic model which he calls "social businesses." Unlike traditional profit-motivated businesses, the objective of a social business is to provide a good or services which will improve the lives of those who purchase it – at a price which covers only the costs of production. Although run like traditional businesses, these companies take any profits which accrue[1] and use them either to lower the price of their product, or to reinvest in another social business, and thereby create a snowball effect of social good. Regarding globalization, Yunus argues that technology provides the very poorest nations not only with the opportunity to participate in the world marketplace, but the advantage of being able to build a cutting-edge infrastructure for their emerging economies. In addition, he notes that the challenges presented by globalization will demand that we think about our planet and its population in a more environmental and social way. You can watch an interview with Muhammad Yunus at: http://www.youtube.com/watch?v=GWZb-aJM1Pk.

[1] to accrue: to accumulate, to acquire

Creating a World Without Poverty[2]

by Muhammad Yunus

As we are all witnessing,[3] the world is going through a revolution driven by information technology (IT). Business, government, education, the media – all are being transformed by the Internet, wireless telephony, access to powerful yet inexpensive computing technology, cable and satellite television, and other elements of the new IT. But what is less well understood is the enormous potential of the new IT for transforming the status of the poorest people in the world.

It is not the huge size of the annual addition to the GDP[4] that characterizes the new society being created by the information revolution. It is not about the wealth that certain people or companies are accumulating[5] by using this technology. The new IT's unique contribution comes from one fundamental fact: It is creating new relationships among people. And this transformation will inevitably have a profound impact on the lives of the poor, particularly poor women and children.

How will IT affect the world's poorest economies? Broadly speaking, there are two possibilities.

One possibility is that, with the emergence of new economic forces driven by IT and their ever-increasing strength in the world economy, nations that were small, weak, and poor under the old dispensation[6] will be further marginalized, making it even more difficult for them to compete. Under this scenario, IT will make the current rush toward uncontrolled globalization even stronger and more unstoppable. Global corporations will dictate terms to the weak economies, which will have no choice but to submit. Their role in the new information-driven economy – if any – will be to provide the most menial[7] services and the cheapest, least-differentiated products, while the lion's share[8] of the economic re-

[2] Muhammad Yunus with Karl Weber, *Creating a World Without Poverty: Social Business and the Future of Capitalism*, New York: Public Affairs, 2007, 187–193, 213–216
[3] to witness: to be present and observe s.th. while it is happening
[4] GDP: gross domestic product, the total value of all the goods and services produced by a country in one year
[5] to accumulate: to gather up
[6] dispensation: (here): political system
[7] menial ['mi:niəl]: requiring little mental effort
[8] lion's share (fig.): the largest part

wards will go to their better-educated, richer, more advanced, and more powerful counterparts to the north.

But there is another possibility, one that is just the opposite of the pessimistic scenario. It's possible that the new IT will spread into the sleepy, backward economies of the global South[9] so quickly that they will no longer remain sleepy. If the leaders of the developing world are wise and the people are eager and energetic, the new IT can be turned into a magic wand.[10] The distance- and time-annihilating[11] properties of electronic information management and communications can be used to eliminate many of the barriers that blocked the developing nations from full participation in the global economy. The new IT can become a great leveler, allowing people and companies in countries from Bangladesh to Bolivia to compete on an equal basis with their counterparts in the United States and Europe. It is this second scenario that I believe can and will happen – provided we have the will to make it happen.

There are skeptics who think the poor economies are incapable of using IT as a fulcrum[12] for growth. In this chapter, I'll illustrate how the new IT can enable poor economies to leapfrog past patterns of economic development and become successfully integrated into the world economy much faster than anyone might have predicted. I'll also list some of the practical, concrete steps that can be taken by both the rich countries and the poor to ensure that the benefits of IT are enjoyed by all, including those who today are among the least privileged people in the world.

Globalization is another trend that is transforming our world, both economically and socially. And like IT, it can be either a force for positive change for the poor or yet another way to marginalize and exploit[13] them.

Open markets are crucial[14] to economic growth. Free trade can potentially benefit all peoples. But we need well-designed global rules if we are to achieve this outcome. Without such rules, the richest and most powerful companies and countries will dominate those that are poorer and weaker. Instead, globalization can be managed in such a way that less-developed societies and individuals can find their own place and, in time, catch up to their more powerful neighbors.

---

[9] global South: poorer countries
[10] magic wand: *Zauberstab*
[11] to annihilate: to destroy
[12] fulcrum (fig.): a means or instrument to do s.th.
[13] to exploit: to take advantage of
[14] crucial ['kruːʃl]: very important

If these two trends – the IT revolution and the advance of globalization – are guided into productive channels, a social revolution will take place on the heels of[15] the current revolutions in technology and economics. There will be an unprecedented explosion in the personal and economic freedom enjoyed by humans around the globe.

Two groups that can play an important role in this revolution and will be among its main beneficiaries are women and youth. Newly empowered to unleash[16] the creativity that has formerly been repressed, these two groups can lead the world toward a new era of growth and prosperity. It's the job of the current generation of leaders to ensure that this happens.

The Power of IT to Help the Poor

In several major areas, IT can play a powerful role in bringing an end to poverty. Here are some of the unique[17] capabilities of the new IT for serving the world's poorest:

- The new IT can help to integrate the poor in the process of globalization by expanding their markets through e-commerce. Traditionally, the poor have been victimized by middlemen who have controlled their access to markets, dictated business terms, and siphoned off[18] profits. Properly applied, the new IT can largely eliminate middlemen who fail to add unique value, allowing people in the poorest countries to work directly with consumers in the developed world and creating international job opportunities through electronically enabled outsourcing.

- The new IT can promote self-employment among the poor, liberating them from reliance on corporate employers or government make-work programs[19] and unleashing their creativity, energy, and productivity. Armed[20] with a cell phone and an Internet connection, a Bangladeshi villager can launch an enterprise that serves customers in Dhaka or

[15] on the heels of: following immediately after
[16] to unleash: to set free
[17] unique: one of a kind
[18] to siphon ['saɪfn] off: to remove
[19] make-work program: program that creates jobs
[20] armed: equipped

Mumbai, London or New York, transcending the vagaries[21] of local economic fluctuations and market conditions.

- The new IT can bring education, knowledge, and skill training to the poor in a very friendly way. One huge barrier to economic advancement for those in the developing countries has been the sheer difficulty, cost, and inconvenience of bringing teachers, consultants, and other suppliers of outside expertise into remote villages that are separated from capital cities by mountains, rivers, jungles, deserts, or hundreds of kilometers of inadequate roads. For many purposes, the Internet eliminates such barriers, making it possible, for example, for a dairy farmer in a remote region of Bangladesh or Peru to consult with an agricultural expert in Beijing or Chicago about the latest techniques for improving the health of his cattle and increasing their yield.[22]

The best aspect of the new IT is that it cannot be controlled by a single owner or authority. It is an empowering tool that enhances options and brings all the world's knowledge to everyone's doorstep. When IT enters a poor economy, it creates wider choices and new relationships, replacing the traditional uni-directional relationship between the rich and poor with a set of multi-dimensional and global relationships in which the poor have an equal footing.

Many people in the developed world believe that IT is totally irrelevant to the problems of poor people. According to this view, IT is too complicated, too expensive, and too impractical for the poor.

This attitude sounds hard-headed[23] and sensible at the abstract level. Yet I've experienced the power of visionary technology to transform the lives of the very poor – in the face of negative predictions by the skeptics.

When we launched our cell-phone company, Grameen Phone, in 1996, the skeptics essentially said, "You must be crazy to think of selling cell phones to poor, illiterate women in the villages of Bangladesh. None of them have even seen a conventional telephone in their lives! They can't afford a phone, they won't know how to dial a number, and anyway whom will they call? The whole idea is insane! You should stick to what you know, and leave the high-tech stuff to the big corporations and the engineering experts."

---

[21] vagaries (plural): changes that are difficult to predict or control
[22] yield: the amount produced
[23] hard-headed: practical or realistic

Yet the Grameen telephone ladies have emerged as a major force for social, economic, and technological transformation in Bangladesh. They are serving as information lifelines for their villages and creating businesses that benefit themselves and their families. Their telephones also provide Internet services. They are now moving in the direction of becoming "Internet ladies" as well. As the technology continues to evolve, they will be the first ones to bring the super-powerful digital genie[24] into the remote, once-isolated villages of Bangladesh, helping their neigh-

"To survive in the new global economy will require massive consistent effort and immediate bold action! Without further delay, I am putting together a 10 year plan to study the problem further."

bors solve problems and discover opportunities formerly reserved for the highly educated and the wealthy. Through the Internet, the villagers will gain access to all the information, services, and economic networks of the world.

As for those who doubt the ability of poor, illiterate women to play such a role: I remember asking some of the very first batch[25] of telephone ladies, "Do you have any difficulty dialing telephone numbers?"

They all told me that they had no such problem. One stood up and declared, "Put a blindfold on me and tell me a number to dial! If I can't

[24] genie ['dʒi:ni]: *Flaschengeist*
[25] batch: group

dial it correctly the very first time, I'll turn in my phone and get out of the business."

I was astounded[26] by her confidence in her newfound skill. But this is what happens when you give the poor an opportunity to show what they can do – almost always, they seize[27] the opportunity and run with it.

Already another Grameen company (Grameen Communications) is setting up Internet kiosks in the villages and running them on a commercial basis. We've been pleasantly surprised to see the response from the villagers to the opportunity to use the Internet and other computer services. Many young people are signing up to learn computer skills for a modest fee.[28] In villages that the national electrical grid[29] doesn't reach, solar panels marketed by Grameen Shakti are powering the cell phones and computers.

Both Microcredit and IT can empower poor people, particularly poor women, in ways that go far beyond what dollars and cents can measure. I am convinced that the best way to combat poverty is to give dignity[30] and self-reliance to poor women. Both IT and Microcredit do this very effectively and mutually[31] reinforce each other in the effort.

This is not to say that the challenges raised by the skeptics are completely wrong. The ability of the poor and the illiterate to afford and use the new IT depends on the appropriateness[32] of the institutional environment around the poor and the rate of return on the investment they must make. Microcredit can provide an appropriately supportive institutional environment, as demonstrated by the success of the thousands of village phone ladies who purchased their equipment through loans from Grameen Bank and have transformed their small bits of technology into thriving local businesses.

Another misconception is that developing nations must recapitulate[33] the path of development followed by developed countries decades or even centuries ago. New technologies hold out the potential for leapfrogging steps in the process. It is not necessary for a developing country in Asia, Africa, or Latin America to build a network of land lines to provide telephone service, as was done in Europe and North America in the

[26] to astonish: to amaze
[27] to seize: to take quickly
[28] modest fee: small amount of money
[29] grid: *Netz*
[30] dignity: sense of self-worth
[31] mutually: directed by each toward the other
[32] appropriateness: suitability
[33] to recapitulate: to do over in the same manner

late nineteenth and early twentieth centuries. Instead, those regions can jump directly to wireless cellular telephone service, saving vast amounts of money, years of development time, and precious nonrenewable resources (such as the copper once used in making telephone lines) in the process.

China, India, Bangladesh, and many other countries have made exactly this leap. Cell-phone outreach is expanding in these countries like a tidal wave.[34] Now the real challenge is to discover all the many ways these phones can improve the lives of the people who own them.

Similarly, it may not be necessary for a developing country to go through a heavy industry phase in which businesses like steel, autos, and machinery are emphasized. Instead, such a country may be able to develop its economy around information-age technologies such as software development, IT support services, and production of a host[35] of consumer goods. Fresh, unprejudiced thinking reveals a range of such opportunities for integrating the developing countries into the world economy with amazing speed and effectiveness.

[...]

Making Space for a New Set of Voices

Today the marketplace is dominated by the voices of traditional capitalism. Many of these voices speak on behalf of corporations, urging consumers through advertising, marketing, publicity, and consumption-oriented media (such as magazines devoted to cars, fashion, home decorating, and vacations) to buy more goods and services as quickly as they can. The sole messages are: Buy More! Buy More! Buy More! And Buy Now! Buy Now! Buy Now! And we wonder why so many young people are alienated,[36] and why older people often feel their lives have been less than fully satisfying.

The only voice in the marketplace is the voice of profit-maximizing businesses, geared to[37] making sure that the objective of ever-increasing consumption is achieved. This voice follows consumers everywhere – when they are reading newspapers, listening to the radio, watching TV, driving their cars, or surfing the Internet. A seamless stream of messages

[34] tidal wave: very large wave that hits the shore
[35] host: a great number
[36] alienated ['eɪliəneɪtɪd]: feeling that you don't belong
[37] geared to: designed or organized to achieve a certain purpose

urging consumption keeps flowing every second of their waking hours. Businesses are finding ever smarter ways to grab consumers' attention in every possible situation and persuade them to buy their products. No wonder virtually everyone finally surrenders and makes the purchase. But even then the commercial propaganda does not stop. Businesses then want consumers to buy more, to abandon the first product in favor of a newer, more expensive model, or to buy more simply for the sake[38] of buying.

This process of promoting consumption is supposed to be a driving force behind economic growth. But what about global sustainability?[39] What about restraining wasteful consumption? What about the personal satisfaction to be derived from enjoying what one has rather than constantly striving[40] to seize the lead in an endless struggle for economic dominance? Don't these values deserve a hearing, too?

I strongly feel that we need a parallel voice in the marketplace, offering consumers a different set of messages – messages like:

- Think about whether you really need it!
- The more you buy, the more likely it is that you are exhausting[41] earth's nonrenewable resources.
- Check the packaging – is it wasteful?
- Buy from a company that will take back your last purchase and recycle it.
- Create a socially responsible home.
- Are you spending like a citizen of the world?

Where the voice of the PMB[42] urges consumers to damage their health through excessive consumption ("Why not super-size it?"),[43] the parallel voice will send messages about the pleasures of being healthy and the steps required to achieve good health: what to eat and what not to eat, how to help kids become interested in nutritious[44] foods, how exercise and activity contribute[45] to well-being, why natural and locally produced foods taste better and are better for you, and so on.

---

[38] sake: purpose
[39] sustainability: using natural resources and renewable energy so as not to harm the environment
[40] to strive: to try
[41] to exhaust: to use up
[42] PMB: profit maximizing business
[43] to super-size: to order a larger portion
[44] nutritious [nju'trɪʃəs]: healthy
[45] to contribute: to add to s.th.

Some might complain that I am urging the use of "propaganda" to manipulate people, or that I am trying to turn society into a "nanny" that nags[46] people about proper[47] behavior. But the people of the world are already being inundated[48] by propaganda and by the nagging of a nanny – except the propaganda and the nagging come from the corporate profit-makers, whose only motive in spending huge sums of money is to cajole[49] consumers into providing them with even bigger profits. We need a parallel voice to provide at least a semblance[50] of balance.

Where will this parallel voice come from? Social business can play a crucial role. Even today, parallel voices like the one I've described are available. They come from schools, NGOs,[51] charities,[52] foundations, faith groups, and other not-for-profit organizations. But these voices are faint[53] and hard to hear. Short on money, the groups that provide these voices lack the giant platform and the powerful media megaphone that mainstream businesses enjoy. No wonder they reach only a tiny audience and are generally drowned out by pro-consumption hype.[54]

If this voice comes from mainstream business as a business message in a business campaign format, it will reach a much bigger audience. An important part of the campaign will be to make social business understood and appreciated by people. I believe that the core[55] idea of social business is already embedded in every human mind, waiting to find expression – only our existing theoretical framework does not recognize it.

As I travel the globe speaking about microcredit and social business, I've met countless young people in schools, colleges, and universities throughout the world. I've been impressed by their idealism, their compassion, and their creativity. I believe they are ready and willing to do the right things for themselves and for the world.

Social businesses may become a source of the strong counter-voice that we are looking for. They can be a credible source that people can believe, because they know that those who speak aren't trying to manipulate them in search of personal gain.

---

[46] to nag: to constantly urge s.o. to do s.th. in an annoying way
[47] proper: correct
[48] to inundate: to flood
[49] to cajole [kəˈdʒəʊl]: to persuade by being nice
[50] semblance: appearance
[51] NGO: non-governmental organization
[52] charity: organization to help the poor
[53] faint: weak
[54] hype [haɪp]: exaggerated praise
[55] core: central

A social business dedicated[56] to environmental objectives can highlight how PMBs are harming the planet and how consumers can alleviate[57] the climate crisis by using environmentally friendly products. A social business running a microcredit program can explain why this program is necessary and how the mainstream banking system needs to be reformed. A social business offering low-cost health insurance can inform people about ways of staying healthy without spending money on doctors or medications, through preventive care, sound[58] nutrition, and exercise. Providing consumers with unbiased advice and information can itself be an attractive area of social business.

Because social businesses are, above all, businesses, they will have the incentive,[59] the resources, and the market clout[60] necessary to bring their out-of-the-mainstream messages to a broad, mainstream audience for the first time. And social businesses will have a competitive advantage in the marketplace of ideas because everyone will know they have no incentive to lie. Because there are no dividend-takers in a social business, the only objective of the company is to create a social benefit. Consumers who hear about the cause and share the values behind it will support the business – and spread the message.

The voice of social business will find ready listeners because many people feel harassed,[61] abused,[62] and manipulated by the marketing techniques applied by PMBs. Many people, particularly the young, will listen because they want to find a way of life that is healthy, sustainable, environmentally friendly, generous[63] to the poor, and conducive[64] to peace of mind.

The ultimate result, as the efforts of thousands of social businesses accumulate,[65] will be an unmistakable shift in the tone and content of the public conversation. Values other than money will have a place in the discussion and be recognized for what they are: important guides and stepping stones toward a more meaningful and satisfying life.

[56] dedicated to: committed to *(engagiert)*
[57] to alleviate: to lessen
[58] sound: sensible
[59] incentive: something which encourages certain decisions or actions
[60] clout [klaʊt]: influence
[61] to harass: to constantly annoy, to continuously put under pressure
[62] to abuse: to mistreat
[63] generous: liberal in giving
[64] conducive: promoting
[65] to accumulate: to build up

Richard Florida was born in Newark, New Jersey in 1957. He received his Bachelor's degree from Rutgers College and a Ph.D. from Columbia University. A professor at the University of Toronto, he is also senior editor of *The Atlantic* and a global best-selling author, famous for his provocative views on how creativity is revolutionizing the global economy. Florida's ideas on the "creative class," commercial innovation, and regional development have been featured in major ad campaigns from BMW and Apple, and are being used globally to change the way regions and nations do business and transform their economies. He has also been appointed to the Business Innovation Factory's Research Advisory Council and recently named European Ambassador for Creativity and Innovation. One of the world's most sought after speakers on global trends, economics, prosperity, competitiveness and growth, Florida was recently named one of *Esquire Magazine's* Best and Brightest, alongside luminaries[1] such as Bill Clinton and Jeffrey Sachs. He lives with his wife in Toronto.

In the excerpts below, Florida describes the rise of what he calls the creative class – the ever increasing number of people whose jobs require their creative participation. The driving force behind the global economy, the values, lifestyles, and buying power of this class is having a dramatic impact on our societies. One example is that, more than simply accepting the best paid job offer they get, members of this class take into consideration where the job is located and what that place has to offer with regard to their creative lifestyles. Urban and economic planners have come to take this idea very seriously, with local governments devoting[2] resources that will make their cities and regions culturally and environmentally appealing in order to attract such creative talent, as well as the companies that seek to employ them. You can watch an interview with Richard Florida at: http://www.youtube.com/watch?v=F6LyyjzYuFU.

[1] luminary: famous person

[2] to devote: (here): to invest

The Rise of the Creative Class[3]

by Richard Florida

Something's happening here but you don't know what it is, do you, Mr. Jones?

– Bob Dylan

Here's a thought experiment. Take a typical man on the street from the year 1900 and drop him into the 1950s. Then take someone from the 1950s and move him Austin Powers-style[4] into the present day. Who would experience the greater change?

At first glance[5] the answer seems obvious. Thrust[6] forward into the 1950s, a person from the turn of the twentieth century would be awe-struck[7] by a world filled with baffling[8] technological wonders. In place of horse-drawn carriages, he would see streets and highways jammed with cars, trucks and buses. In the cities, immense skyscrapers would line the horizon, and mammoth bridges would span rivers and inlets[9] where once only ferries could cross. Flying machines would soar overhead, carrying people across the continent or the oceans in a matter of hours rather than days. At home, our 1900-to-1950s time-traveler would grope[10] his way through a strange new environment filled with appliances[11] powered by electricity: radios and televisions emanating[12] musical sounds and even human images, refrigerators to keep things cold, washing machines to clean his clothes automatically, and much more. A massive new super-market would replace daily trips to the market with an array[13] of techno-

[3] Richard Florida, *The Rise of the Creative Class*, New York: Basic Books, 2002, 1–11
[4] Austin Powers: the main character in a series of films that parody James Bond
[5] glance: a quick look
[6] to thrust: to push with force
[7] awestruck: amazed
[8] to baffle: to confuse
[9] inlet: bay
[10] to grope: to feel around blindly
[11] appliance: electronic device used in a household
[12] to emanate: to send out
[13] array: group or collection

logically enhanced[14] foods, such as instant coffee or frozen vegetables to put into the refrigerator. Life itself would be dramatically extended. Many once-fatal ailments[15] could be prevented with an injection or cured with a pill. The newness of this time-traveler's physical surroundings – the speed and power of everyday machines – would be profoundly disorienting.

"Well. Yes. We could read your blog ... or you could just tell us about your school day."

On the other hand, someone from the 1950s would have little trouble navigating the physical landscape of today. Although we like to think ours is the age of boundless[16] technological wonders, our second time-traveler would find himself in a world not all that different from the one he left. He would still drive a car to work. If he took the train, it would likely be of the same line leaving from the same station. He could probably board an airplane at the same airport. He might still live in a suburban house though a bigger one. Television would have more channels, but it would basically be the same, and he could still catch some of his favorite 1950 shows on reruns.[17] He would know how, or quickly

[14] to enhance: to improve
[15] ailment ['eɪlmənt]: health problem
[16] boundless: without limits
[17] rerun (colloquial): old programme shown again

learn how, to operate most household appliances – even the personal computer, with its familiar QWERTY keyboard. In fact with just a few exceptions, such as the PC, the Internet, CD and DVD players, the cash machine[18] and a wireless phone he could carry with him, he would be familiar with almost all current-day technology. Perhaps disappointed by the pace of progress, he might ask "Why haven't we conquered[19] outer space?" or "Where are all the robots?"

On the basis of big, obvious technological changes alone, surely the 1900-to-1950s traveler would experience the greater shift, while the other might easily conclude that we'd spent the second half of the twentieth century doing little more than tweaking[20] the great waves of the first half.[21]

But the longer they stayed in their new homes, the more each time-traveler would become aware of subtler dimensions of change. Once the glare of technology had dimmed,[22] each would begin to notice their respective society's changed norms[23] and values, and the ways in which everyday people live and work. And here the tables would be turned.[24] In terms of adjusting to the social structures and the rhythms and patterns of daily life, our second time-traveler would be much more disoriented.

Someone from the early 1900s would find the social world of the 1950 remarkably similar to his own. If he worked in a factory, he might find much the same divisions of labor, the same hierarchical systems of control. If he worked in an office, he would be immersed in the same

[18] cash machine (colloquial): ATM (automated teller machine) from which money can be obtained with a bank card
[19] to conquer: to gain mastery over
[20] to tweak: to make small improvements
[21] [author's note] For a careful empirical comparison of technological change at the turn of the twentieth century versus modern times, see Robert Gordon, "Does the New Economy Measure Up to the Great Inventions of the Past?" Cambridge, Mass.: National Bureau of Economic Research, Working Paper No. 7833, August 2000. His answer is a resounding no. The great majority of the technological inventions in the National Academy of Engineering's "Greatest Engineering Accomplishments of the 20th Century" occurred prior to 1950. Only two of the top ten occurred after World War II (semiconductor electronics, no. 5, and computers, no. 8), while the Internet, the subject of so much New Economy hype, ranks thirteenth. See www.greatachicvements.org.
[22] to dim: to become less bright
[23] norms: set of standards
[24] to turn the tables: to reverse

bureaucracy, the same climb up the corporate ladder. He would come to work at 8 or 9 each morning and leave promptly at 5, his life neatly segmented into compartments of home and work. He would wear a suit and tie. Most of his business associates would be white and male. Their values and office politics would hardly have changed. He would seldom see women in the work place, except as secretaries, and almost never interact professionally with someone of another race. He would marry young, have children quickly thereafter, stay married to the same person and probably work for the same company for the rest of his life. In his leisure time, he'd find that movies and TV had largely superseded[25] live stage shows, but otherwise his recreational activities would be much the same as they were in 1900: taking in[26] a baseball game or a boxing match, maybe playing a round of golf. He would join the clubs and civic groups befitting[27] his socioeconomic class, observe the same social distinctions, and fully expect his children to do likewise. The tempo of his life would be structured by the values and norms of organizations. He would find himself living the life of the "company man" so aptly chronicled[28] by writers from Sinclair Lewis and John Kenneth Galbraith to William Whyte and C. Wright Mills.[29]

Our second time-traveler, however, would be quite unnerved by the dizzying[30] social and cultural changes that had accumulated between the 1950s and today. At work he would find a new dress code, a new schedule, and new rules. He would see office workers dressed like folks relaxing on the weekend, in jeans and open-necked shirts, and be shocked to learn they occupy[31] positions of authority. People at the of-

[25] to supersede: to replace
[26] to take in: to go and see s.th.
[27] befitting: appropriate to
[28] aptly chronicled: well documented
[29] [author's note] Among the most popular, indeed classic works in this vein, see Sinclair Lewis, *Main Street*. New York: Harcourt, Brace and Company, 1920; and *Babbitt*. New York: Harcourt, Brace and World, 1922; William H. Whyte, Jr., *The Organization Man*. New York: Simon and Schuster, 1956; David Riesman, *The Lonely Crowd: A Study of the Changing American Character*. New Haven: Yale University Press, 1950; C. Wright Mills, *White Collar: The American Middle Classes*. New York: Oxford University Press, 1951; John Kenneth Galbraith, *The New Industrial State*. New York: Houghton-Mifflin, 1967. Also see Anthony Sampson, *Company Man: The Rise and Fall of Corporate Life*. New York: Times Books, 1995.
[30] dizzying: confusing
[31] to occupy: to fill

fice would seemingly come and go as they pleased.[32] The younger ones might sport bizarre piercings and tattoos. Women and even nonwhites would be managers. Individuality and self-expression would be valued over conformity to organizational norms – and yet these people would seem strangely puritanical to this time-traveler. His ethnic jokes would fall embarrassingly flat.[33] His smoking would get him banished to the parking lot, and his two-martini lunches would raise genuine concern. Attitudes and expressions he had never thought about would cause repeated offense.[34] He would continually suffer the painful feeling of not knowing how to behave.

Out on the street, this time-traveler would see different ethnic groups in greater numbers than he ever could have imagined – Asian-, Indian-, and Latin-Americans and others – all mingling[35] in ways he found strange and perhaps inappropriate. There would be mixed-race couples, and same-sex couples carrying the upbeat-sounding moniker[36] "gay?" While some of these people would be acting in familiar ways – a woman shopping while pushing a stroller,[37] an office worker having lunch at a counter –others, such as grown men clad[38] in form-fitting gear whizzing by on high-tech bicycles, or women on strange new roller skates with their torsos covered only by "brassières"[39] – would appear to be engaged in alien activities.

People would seem to be always working and yet never working when they were supposed to. They would strike him as lazy and yet obsessed with exercise. They would seem career-conscious yet fickle[40] – doesn't anybody stay with the company more than three years? – and caring yet anti-social: What happened to the ladies' clubs, Moose Lodges[41] and

[32] pleased: (here): wanted
[33] to fall flat: to not produce a laugh
[34] to cause offense: to insult
[35] to mingle: to interact
[36] moniker: label
[37] stroller (AE): pushchair (BE)
[38] to be clad: to be clothed
[39] brassière ['bræziə] (formal): bra: piece of clothing women use to support their breasts
[40] fickle: constantly changing your mind
[41] Moose Lodge: any building and meeting place of Moose International, an international club of men and women

bowling leagues? While the physical surroundings would be relatively familiar, the feel of the place would be bewilderingly[42] different.

Thus, although the first time-traveler had to adjust to some drastic technological changes, it is the second who experiences the deeper, more pervasive[43] transformation. It is the second who has been thrust into a time when lifestyles and worldviews are most assuredly changing – a time when the old order has broken down, when flux[44] and uncertainty themselves seem to be part of the everyday norm.

The Force Behind the Shift

What caused this transformation? What happened between the 1950s and today that did not happen in the earlier period? Scholars and pundits[45] have floated[46] many theories, along with a range of opinions on whether the changes are good or bad. Some bemoan[47] the passing of traditional social and cultural forms, while others point to a rosy future based largely on new technology. Yet on one point most of them agree. Most tend to see the transformation as something that's being done to us unwittingly.[48] Some complain that certain factions of society have imposed[49] their values on the rest of us; others say that our own inventions are turning around to reshape us. They're wrong.

Society is changing in large measure because we want it to. Moreover, it is changing neither in random chaotic ways nor in some mysterious collective-unconscious way, but in ways that are perfectly sensible and rational. The logic behind the transformation has been unclear to this point because the transformation is still in progress. But lately a number of diverse and seemingly unconnected threads are starting to come together. The deeper pattern, the force behind the shift, can now be discerned.[50]

---

[42] bewilderingly: confusingly
[43] pervasive: spreading through every part
[44] flux: change
[45] pundit: person who offers his or her opinion through the media
[46] to float: (here): to propose
[47] to bemoan: to complain
[48] unwittingly: unconsciously
[49] to impose: to force
[50] to discern: to understand, to recognize

That driving force is the rise of human creativity as the key factor in our economy and society. Both at work and in other spheres of our lives, we value creativity more highly than ever, and cultivate it more intensely. The creative impulse – the attribute that distinguishes us, as humans, from other species – is now being let loose on an unprecedented scale. The purpose of this book is to examine how and why this is so, and to trace[51] its effects as they ripple through our world.

Consider first the realm of economics. Many say that we now live in an "information" economy or a "knowledge" economy. But what's more fundamentally true is that we now have an economy powered by human creativity. Creativity – "the ability to create meaningful new forms," as Webster's[52] dictionary puts it – is now the decisive source of competitive advantage. In virtually every industry, from automobiles to fashion, food products, and information technology itself, the winners in the long run are those who can create and keep creating. This has always been true, from the days of the Agricultural Revolution to the Industrial Revolution. But in the past few decades we've come to recognize it clearly and act upon it systematically.

Creativity is multidimensional and comes in many mutually reinforcing forms. It is a mistake to think, as many do, that creativity can be reduced to the creation of new blockbuster inventions, new products and new firms. In today's economy creativity is pervasive and ongoing: We constantly revise[53] and enhance every product, process and activity imaginable, and fit them together in new ways. Moreover, technological and economic creativity are nurtured[54] by and interact with artistic and cultural creativity. This kind of interplay is evident in the rise of whole new industries from computer graphics to digital music and animation. Creativity also requires a social and economic environment that can nurture its many forms. Max Weber[55] said long ago that the Protestant ethic provided the underlying spirit of thrift,[56] hard work and efficiency that motivated the rise of early capitalism. In similar fashion, the shared

[51] to trace: to follow
[52] Webster: major American dictionary publisher
[53] to revise: to make changes to s.th.
[54] to nurture: to help grow
[55] Max Weber (1864–1920): German economist and sociologist, best known for *The Protestant Ethic and the Spirit of Capitalism* (1904–1905)
[56] thrift: habit of saving money and spending it carefully

commitment to the creative spirit in its many, varied manifestations underpins[57] the new creative ethos that powers our age.

Thus creativity has come to be the most highly prized commodity in our economy – and yet it is not a "commodity." Creativity comes from people. And while people can be hired and fired, their creative capacity cannot be bought and sold, or turned on and off at will.[58] This is why, for instance, we see the emergence of a new order in the workplace. Hiring for diversity, once a matter of legal compliance,[59] has become a matter of eco survival because creativity comes in all colors, genders[60] and personal preferences. Schedules, rules and dress codes have become more flexible to cater[61] to how the creative process works. Creativity must be motivated and nurtured in a multitude of ways, by employers, by people themselves and by the communities where they locate. Small wonder that we find the creative ethos bleeding out from the sphere of work to infuse[62] every corner of our lives.

At the same time, entirely new forms of economic infrastructure, such as systematic spending on research and development, the high-tech start-up company and an extensive system of venture finance, have evolved to support creativity and mobilize creative people around promising[63] ideas and products. Capitalism has also expanded its reach to capture the talents of heretofore[64] excluded groups of eccentrics and nonconformists. In doing so, it has pulled off yet another astonishing mutation: taking people who would once have been viewed as bizarre mavericks[65] operating at the bohemian fringe[66] and setting them at the very heart of the process of innovation and economic growth. These changes in the economy and in the workplace have in turn helped to propagate[67] and legitimize similar changes in society at large. The creative individual is no longer viewed as an iconoclast. He – or she – is the new mainstream.

---

57 to underpin: to support
58 at will: when one wants
59 to comply: to fulfill a requirement
60 gender: sexual category
61 to cater: to provide what is needed
62 to infuse: to fill
63 promising: likely to succeed
64 heretofore: up until now
65 maverick: individual with unusual, independent ideas
66 Bohemian fringe: unconventional edges of society
67 to propagate: to spread

In tracing economic shifts, I often say that our economy is moving from an older corporate-centered system defined by large companies to a more people-driven one. This view should not be confused with the unfounded and silly notion that big companies are dying off. Nor do I buy the fantasy of an economy organized around small enterprises and independent "free agents." Companies, including very big ones, obviously still exist, are still influential and probably always will be. I simply mean to stress that as the fundamental source of creativity, people are the critical resource of the new age. This has far-reaching effects – for instance, on our economic and social geography and the nature of our communities.

It's often been said that in this age of high technology, "geography is dead" and place doesn't matter anymore. Nothing could be further from the truth: Witness how high-tech firms themselves concentrate in specific places like the San Francisco Bay Area or Austin or Seattle. Place has become the central organizing unit of our time, taking on many of the functions that used to be played by firms and other organizations. Corporations have historically played a key economic role in matching people to jobs, particularly given the long-term employment system of the post–World War II era. But today corporations are far less committed to their employees and people change jobs frequently, making the employment contract more contingent.[68] In this environment, it is geographic place rather than the corporation that provides the organizational matrix[69] for matching people and jobs. Access to talented and creative people is to modern business what access to coal and iron ore was to steelmaking. It determines where companies will choose to locate and grow, and this in turn changes the ways cities must compete. As Hewlett-Packard CEO Carley Fiorina once told this nation's governors: "Keep your tax incentives and highway interchanges; we will go where the highly skilled people are."

Creative people, in turn, don't just cluster[70] where the jobs are. They cluster in places that are centers of creativity and also where they like to live. From classical Athens and Rome, to the Florence of the Medici and Elizabethan London, to Greenwich Village and the San Francisco

[68] contingent: dependent on other factors
[69] matrix: environment or setting out of which s.th. develops
[70] to cluster: to group

Bay Area, creativity has always gravitated[71] to specific locations. As the great urbanist[72] Jane Jacobs[73] pointed out long ago, successful places are multidimensional and diverse – they don't just cater to a single industry or a single demographic group; they are full of stimulation and creativity interplay. In my consulting work, I often tell business and political leaders that places need a people climate – or a creativity climate – as well as a business climate. Cities like Seattle, Austin, Toronto and Dublin recognize the multidimensional nature of this transformation and are striving to become broadly creative communities, not just centers of technological innovation and high-tech industry. If places like Buffalo, Grand Rapids, Memphis and Louisville do not follow suit,[74] they will be hard-pressed to survive.

Our fundamental social forms are shifting as well, driven by forces traceable to the creative ethos. In virtually every aspect of life, weak ties[75] have replaced the stronger bonds[76] that once gave structure to society. Rather than live in one town for decades, we now move about. Instead of communities defined by close associations and deep commitments to family, friends and organizations, we seek places where we can make friends and acquaintances easily and live quasi-anonymous lives. The decline in the strength of our ties to people and institutions is a product of the increasing number of ties we have. As a retired[77] industrialist who was the head of a technology transfer center in Ottawa, Canada, told me: "My father grew up in a small town and worked for the same company. He knew the same fourteen people in his entire life. I meet more people than that in any given day."[78] Modern life is increasingly defined by contingent[79] commitments. We progress from job to job with amazingly little concern or effort. Where people once found themselves bound together by social institutions and formed their identities in groups, a fundamental

[71] to gravitate: to move toward
[72] urbanist: someone who studies urban environments
[73] Jane Jacobs (1916–2006): American-Canadian writer and activist, best known for her protests against the destruction of established communities threatened by urban renewal policies – Cf. her classic work on the themes mentioned here, *The Death and Life of Great American Cities* (1961)
[74] to follow suit: to do the same
[75] tie: connection
[76] bond: link
[77] retired: having ended one's career due to age
[78] [author's note] Personal interview by author, Ottawa, Canada, September 2001.
[79] contingent: temporary, short-lived

characteristic of life today is that we strive to create our own identities.[80] It is this creation and re-creation of the self, often in ways that reflect our creativity, that is a key feature of the creative ethos.

In this new world, it is no longer the organizations we work for, churches, neighborhoods or even family ties that define us. Instead, we do this ourselves, defining our identities along the varied dimensions of our creativity. Other aspects of our lives – what we consume, new forms of leisure and recreation, efforts at community-building – then organize themselves around this process of identity creation.

Furthermore, when we think about group identity in this new world, we must rethink our notions of class. We often tend to classify people on the basis of their consumption habits or lifestyle choices, or, more crudely,[81] by their income level. For instance, we often equate[82] middle income with middle class. Though I view these things as significant markers of class, they are not its primary determinants. A class is a cluster of people who have common interests and tend to think, feel and behave similarly, but these similarities are fundamentally determined by economic function – by the kind of work they do for a living. All the other distinctions follow from that. And a key fact of our age is that more of us than ever are doing creative work for a living.

The New Class

The economic need for creativity has registered itself in the rise of a new class, which I call the Creative Class. Some 38 million Americans, 30 percent of all employed people, belong to this new class. I define the core of the Creative Class to include people in science and engineering, architecture and design, education, arts, music and entertainment, whose economic function is to create new ideas, new technology and/or new creative content. Around the core, the Creative Class also includes a broader group of creative professionals in business and finance, law, health care and related fields. These people engage in complex problem solving that involves a great deal of independent judgment and requires

---

[80] [author's note] On this point see Manuel Castells, *The Power of Identity: The Information Age: Economy, Society, and Culture, Volume I* Oxford: Blackwell Publishers Ltd., 1997

[81] crudely: (here): not very accurately

[82] to equate: to treat as comparable

high levels of education or human capital. In addition, all members of the Creative Class – whether they are artists or engineers, musicians or computer scientists, writers or entrepreneurs – share a common creative ethos that values creativity, individuality, difference and merit.[83] For the members of the Creative Class, every aspect and every manifestation of creativity – technological, cultural and economic – is interlinked and inseparable.

The key difference between the Creative Class and other classes lies in what they are primarily paid to do. Those in the Working Class and the Service Class are primarily paid to execute according to plan, while those in the Creative Class are primarily paid to create and have considerably more autonomy and flexibility than the other two classes to do so. There are gray areas and boundary issues in my scheme of things, to be sure. And while some may quibble[84] with my definition of the Creative Class and the numerical estimates that are based on it, I believe it has a good deal more precision than existing, more amorphous[85] definitions of knowledge workers, symbolic analysts or professional and technical workers.

The class structure of the United States and other advanced nations has been the subject of great debate for well over a century. For a host of writers in the 1800s and 1900s, the big story was the rise, and then the decline, of the Working Class.[86] For writers like Daniel Bell[87] and others in the middle to later 1900s, a second big story was the rise of a postindustrial society in which many of us shifted from making goods to delivering services. The big story unfolding[88] now – one that has been unfolding for some time – is the rise of the Creative Class, the great emerging class of our time.

The reason modern society feels so different to our time-traveler is the staggering[89] growth of this class. Over the twentieth century, the

---

[83] merit: achievement

[84] to quibble: to argue about small details

[85] amorphous: without clear boarders

[86] [author's note] The classic statement here is that of Karl Marx in both *Capital* and *The Communist Manifesto* among his many other works.

[87] [author's note] Daniel Bell (1919–2011): American sociologist – Cf. *The Coming of Post-Industrial Society*, 1973.

[88] to unfold: to develop

[89] staggering: so great that it is difficult to believe

Creative Class grew from roughly 3 million workers to its current size, a tenfold-plus increase; since 1980 alone it has more than doubled. Roughly 15 million Americans, more than 12 percent of the workforce, compose the Super-Creative Core of this new class. The Creative Class in the United States today is larger than the traditional Working Class – for instance those who work in manufacturing, construction and transportation industries.

The long sweep[90] of the twentieth century has seen the rise and fall of the Working Class, which peaked at roughly 40 percent of the U.S. workforce between 1920 and 1950 before beginning its long slide to roughly a quarter of the workforce today. The Service Class, which includes fields such as personal care, food service and clerical[91] work, has grown steadily over the same period, doubling from roughly 16 to 30 percent of the workforce between 1900 and 1950 before climbing to more than 45 percent by 1980. With some 55 million members today it is the largest class in terms of sheer numbers.

Although the Creative Class remains somewhat smaller than the Service Class, its crucial economic role makes it the most influential. The Creative Class is also considerably larger than the class of "organization men" described in William Whyte's 1956 book. Like Whyte's managerial class, which "set the American temper"[92] in the 1950s, the Creative Class is the norm-setting class of our time. But its norms are very different: Individuality, self-expression and openness to difference are favored over the homogeneity, conformity and "fitting in" that defined the organizational age. Furthermore, the Creative Class is dominant in terms of wealth and income, with its members earning nearly twice as much on average as members of the other two classes.

But the sacrifices we will make for money are very different from those once made by Whyte's organization men. Very few of us work for the same large company or organization for life, and we are far less likely to pin[93] our identity or sense of self-worth on whom we work for. We balance financial considerations against the ability to be ourselves, set our own schedules, do challenging work and live in communities that reflect

---

[90] sweep: (here): course
[91] clerical: administrative
[92] temper: mood
[93] to pin: to connect

our values and priorities. According to one large-scale survey of people who work in information technology fields – a relatively conservative subgroup of the Creative Class –challenge and responsibility, the ability to work a flexible schedule and a secure and stable work environment all rank ahead of money as the key elements of what people value in their jobs. The upheaval[94] in our private lives is epitomized by one well-publicized statistic: Fewer than one-quarter of all Americans (23.5 percent) accounted for by the 2000 Census lived in a "conventional" nuclear family, down from 45 percent in 1960.[95] These profound changes are not, as commonly portrayed, signs of the reckless[96] self-indulgence[97] of a spoiled[98] people. They are undergirded[99] by a simple economic rationality. We live by our creativity, so we try to take care of it and seek environments that allow it to flourish – much as the blacksmith[100] once cared for his forge,[101] and farmers took care of the oxen that drove their plows.[102]

Creativity in the world of work is not limited to members of the Creative Class. Factory workers and even the lowest-end service workers always have been creative in certain valuable ways. Also, the creative content of many working-class and service-class jobs is growing – a prime example being the continuous-improvement programs on many factory floors, which call on line[103] workers to contribute ideas as well as their physical labor. On the basis of these trends, I expect that the Creative Class, which is still emergent, will continue to grow in coming decades, as more traditional economic functions are transformed into Creative Class occupations.[104] And, as the last chapter of this book will argue, I strongly believe that the key to improving the lot of underpaid, underemployed and disadvantaged people lies not in social welfare programs or low-end make-work jobs – nor in somehow bringing back the

[94] upheaval: dramatic change
[95] [author's note] "The Changing American Family." *New York Times*, May 15, 2001.
[96] reckless: without caution
[97] self-indulgence: excessive gratification of one's own desires
[98] to spoil: to treat too well
[99] to undergird: to support
[100] blacksmith: person who uses fire to heat metal and then form it
[101] forge: the furnace used by a blacksmith to heat metal
[102] plow (AE): plough (BE); farm machine used to cut into the soil
[103] line: assembly line
[104] occupation: job

factory jobs of the past – but rather in tapping[105] the creativity of these people, paying them appropriately for it and integrating them fully into the Creative Economy.

Not all is rosy in this emerging mainstream of the Creative Age. With no big company to provide security, we bear much more risk than the corporate and working classes of the organizational age did. We experience and often create high levels of mental and emotional stress, at work and at home. We crave[106] flexibility but have less time to pursue the things we truly desire. The technologies that were supposed to liberate us from work have invaded our lives. And though the Creative Class does not have a monopoly on creativity, it certainly has cornered the lion's share of the market[107] for it – while segmenting both the labor market and society in new ways. Significant fault lines[108] are appearing as the values, attitudes and aspirations of the Creative Class inexorably[109] clash[110] with those of the other established classes. Our society may well be splitting into two or three separate types of economies, cultures and communities, with deepening divides of education, occupation and geographic location.

The nation's geographic center of gravity has shifted away from traditional industrial regions toward new axes[111] of creativity and innovation. The Creative Class is strongly oriented to large cities and regions that offer a variety of economic opportunities, a stimulating environment and amenities[112] for every possible lifestyle. The nation's leading creative centers include major East Coast regions like Washington, D.C., Boston and the greater New York region, and leading high-tech centers like the San Francisco Bay area, Seattle and Austin. These places offer something for everyone – vibrant urban districts, abundant natural amenities and comfortable suburban "nerdistans"[113] for techies so inclined.[114] But large

[105] to tap: (here): to make use of s.th.
[106] to crave: to want very much
[107] to corner the market: to dominate
[108] fault line: dividing line
[109] inexorably [ɪn'eksrəbli]: unavoidably
[110] to clash: to come into conflict
[111] axis (plural: axes): central line around which things rotate
[112] amenity: attractive feature
[113] nerdistan (humorous): an area controlled by nerds, i.e. s.o. obsessively interested in s.th.
[114] inclined: tending to be in favor of a particular thing

regions do not have exclusive hold on the members of this new class. Smaller places like Boulder, Colorado and Santa Fe, New Mexico boast significant concentrations of the Creative Class, as do less obvious places like Gainesville, Florida; Provo, Utah; and Huntsville, Alabama.

This remaking of our economic geography is intimately[115] tied to class identity. Today's professionals see themselves as members of a broad creative force, not as corporate officers or organization men. Thus they gravitate to stimulating creative environments – to places that offer not only opportunities and amenities, but openness to diversity, where they feel they can express themselves and validate[116] their identities. They are fleeing working-class strongholds[117] and in many cases avoiding newer but conservative Sunbelt[118] cities – increasingly opting out of[119] places where tradition is more valued and where the social norms of the organizational age still prevail.[120] In fact, many of these places are being almost entirely abandoned by the Creative Class.

One of the most significant fault lines[121] of our age is the growing geographic segregation of the Creative Class and the other classes. The geographic trends I will describe in this book do *not* favor the tightly knit[122] old-style communities that are so often celebrated in our songs, stories and sentimental TV commercials. Moreover, a number of serious social commentators in recent years have urged us to recultivate and rebuild the old forms of "social capital" found in these communities. Such efforts are fruitless,[123] since they fly in the face of[124] today's economic realities. A central task ahead is developing new forms of social cohesion[125] appropriate to the Creative Age.

---

[115] intimately: closely
[116] to validate: to confirm
[117] stronghold: a place dominated by a particular group
[118] Sunbelt: the South and Southwest of the USA
[119] to opt out of: to decide against s.th.
[120] to prevail: to dominate
[121] fault line (fig.): deep dividing line
[122] tightly knit: very close
[123] fruitless: in vain (*vergeblich*)
[124] to fly in the face of: to go against s.th.
[125] cohesion [kəʊˈhiːʒn]: unity

Francis Fukuyama was born in Chicago, Illinois in 1952. He received his B.A. from Cornell University in Classics, and his Ph.D. from Harvard University in Political Science. He was a member of the Political Science Department of the RAND Corporation, on the Policy Planning Staff of the US Department of State, as well as a member of the President's Council on Bioethics. Fukuyama is currently the Olivier Nomellini Senior Fellow at the Freeman Spogli Institute for International Studies at Stanford University and chairman of the editorial board of The American Interest. He has written widely on issues of political and economic development and his book *The End of History* and *The Last Man* has appeared in over twenty foreign editions. He lives in Stanford, California with his wife and has three children.

Considered to be one of the most audacious[1] articles of the twentieth century, Fukuyama's piece has been hotly debated ever since it was first published in 1989, and later expanded into a book. Based on Hegel's[2] theory of history, the title is often misunderstood, referring to the ideological culmination of socio-political development down through human history, rather than the end of a chain of temporal[3] events. Due to the rise of terrorism associated with the 9-11 attacks on the United States, some critics claimed Fukuyama's theory to be discredited. However, the recent uprisings across the Muslim world, often referred to as the "Arab Spring," seem to indicate that peaceful, democratic impulses for change have been more successful and are thus more appealing than their violent, theocratic-based alternatives. Depending on how these developments evolve, Fukuyama's thesis may yet be affirmed. You can watch an interview with Francis Fukuyama at: http://www.youtube.com/watch?v=fisu-9alhMM.

[1] audacious: daring
[2] Georg Wilhelm Friedrich Hegel (1770–1831): German philosopher, who developed his concept of dialectic that had a great influence on Karl Marx
[3] temporal: lasting for a relatively short time

The End of History?[4]

by Francis Fukuyama

In watching the flow of events over the past decade or so, it is hard to avoid the feeling that something very fundamental has happened in world history. The past year has seen a flood of articles commemorating the end of the Cold War, and the fact that "peace" seems to be breaking out in many regions of the world. Most of these analyses lack any larger conceptual framework for distinguishing between what is essential and what is contingent or accidental in world history, and are predictably superficial.[5] If Mr. Gorbachev[6] were ousted[7] from the Kremlin or a new Ayatollah[8] proclaimed the millennium[9] from a desolate[10] Middle Eastern capital, these same commentators would scramble[11] to announce the re-birth of a new era of conflict.

And yet, all of these people sense dimly that there is some larger process at work, a process that gives coherence and order to the daily headlines.[12] The twentieth century saw the developed world descend[13] into a paroxysm[14] of ideological violence, as liberalism contended first with the remnants of absolutism, then bolshevism and fascism, and finally an updated Marxism that threatened to lead to the ultimate apocalypse of nuclear war. But the century that began full of self-confidence in the ultimate triumph of Western liberal democracy seems at its close to be returning full circle to where it started: not to an "end of ideology" or a convergence between capitalism and socialism, as earlier predicted, but to an unabashed[15] victory of economic and political liberalism.

---

[4] Francis Fukuyama, "The End of History?" *The National Interest*, Summer 1989

[5] superficial [ˌsuːpəˈfɪʃl]: shallow, only on the surface

[6] Michael Gorbachev (1931–): Gorbachev was the last head of the Soviet Union until 1991

[7] to oust: to remove

[8] Ayatollah: high ranking expert in Islamic studies – Cf. Ayatollah Khomeini

[9] millennium: (here): the rebirth of fundamentalist Islam

[10] desolate [ˈdeslət]: lacking in hope

[11] to scramble: to hurry

[12] headline: short title of an article in a newspaper

[13] to descend: to go down

[14] paroxysm [ˈpærəkˌsɪzm]: outburst

[15] unabashed: not ashamed or embarrassed when other people would be

The triumph of the West, of the Western *idea*, is evident first of all in the total exhaustion of viable[16] systematic alternatives to Western liberalism. In the past decade, there have been unmistakable changes in the intellectual climate of the world's two largest communist countries, and the beginnings of significant reform movements in both. But this phenomenon extends beyond high politics and it can be seen also in the ineluctable[17] spread of consumerist Western culture in such diverse contexts as the peasants'[18] markets and color television sets now omnipresent throughout China, the cooperative restaurants and clothing stores opened in the past year in Moscow, the Beethoven piped into[19] Japanese department stores, and the rock music enjoyed alike in Prague, Rangoon, and Tehran.

What we may be witnessing is not just the end of the Cold War, or the passing of a particular period of postwar history, but the end of history as such: that is, the end point of mankind's ideological evolution and the universalization of Western liberal democracy as the final form of human government. This is not to say that there will no longer be events to fill the pages of *Foreign Affair's* yearly summaries of international relations, for the victory of liberalism has occurred primarily in the realm of ideas or consciousness and is as yet incomplete in the real or material world. But there are powerful reasons for believing that it is the ideal that will govern the material world *in the long run*. To understand how this is so, we must first consider some theoretical issues concerning the nature of historical change.

I

The notion of the end of history is not an original one. Its best known propagator was Karl Marx, who believed that the direction of historical development was a purposeful one determined by the interplay of material forces, and would come to an end only with the achievement of a communist utopia that would finally resolve all prior[20] contradictions. But the concept of history as a dialectical process with a beginning, a

---

16 viable ['vaɪəbl]: workable
17 ineluctable: unavoidable
18 peasant: small farmer
19 to pipe into: to play over loudspeakers
20 prior: earlier

middle, and an end was borrowed by Marx from his great German predecessor, Georg Wilhelm Friedrich Hegel.

For better or worse, much of Hegel's historicism has become part of our contemporary intellectual baggage.[21] The notion that mankind has progressed through a series of primitive stages of consciousness on his path to the present, and that these stages corresponded to concrete forms of social organization, such as tribal,[22] slave-owning, theocratic, and finally democratic-egalitarian societies, has become inseparable from the modern understanding of man. Hegel was the first philosopher to speak the language of modern social science, insofar[23] as man for him was the product of his concrete historical and social environment and not, as earlier natural right theorists would have it, a collection of more or less fixed "natural" attributes. The mastery and transformation of man's natural environment through the application of science and technology was originally not a Marxist concept, but a Hegelian one. Unlike later historicists whose historical relativism degenerated[24] into relativism *tout court*,[25] however, Hegel believed that history culminated[26] in an absolute moment – a moment in which a final, rational form of society and state became victorious.

It is Hegel's misfortune[27] to be known now primarily as Marx's precursor;[28] and it is our misfortune that few of us are familiar with Hegel's work from direct study, but only as it has been filtered[29] through the distorting[30] lens of Marxism. In France, however, there has been an effort to save Hegel from his Marxist interpreters and to resurrect[31] him as the philosopher who most correctly speaks to our time. Among those modern French interpreters of Hegel, the greatest was certainly Alexandre Kojéve, a brilliant Russian émigré who taught a highly influential series of seminars in Paris in the 1930s at the *Ecole Practique des Hautes*

[21] baggage (colloquial): (here): what we inherit rather than choose
[22] tribal: based on a small, often related group of people
[23] insofar: to the extent
[24] to degenerate: to sink to a lower level
[25] *tout court*: nothing other than
[26] to culminate: to reach its peak
[27] misfortune: bad luck
[28] precursor: that which came before
[29] to filter: to pass through a filter and thereby change the original material
[30] to distort: to change so as to be incorrect
[31] to resurrect: to bring back to life

Etudes.[32] While largely unknown in the United States, Kojéve had a major impact on the intellectual life of the continent. Among his students ranged such future luminaries[33] as Jean-Paul Sartre on the Left and Raymond Aron on the Right; postwar existentialism borrowed many of its basic categories from Hegel via Kojéve.

Kojéve sought to resurrect the Hegel of the *Phenomenology of Mind*, the Hegel who proclaimed history to be at an end in 1806. For as early as this Hegel saw in Napoleon's defeat of the Prussian monarchy at the Battle of Jena the victory of the ideals of the French Revolution, and the imminent[34] universalization of the state incorporating the principles of liberty and equality. Kojéve, far from rejecting[35] Hegel in light of the turbulent events of the next century and a half, insisted that the latter[36] had been essentially correct.[37] The Battle of Jena marked the end of history because it was at that point that the *vanguard* of humanity (a term quite familiar to Marxists) actualized the principles of the French Revolution. While there was considerable work to be done after 1806 – abolishing slavery and the slave trade, extending the franchise[38] to workers, women, blacks, and other racial minorities, etc. – the basic principles of the liberal democratic state could not be improved upon. The two world wars in this century and their attendant[39] revolutions and upheavals simply had the effect of extending those principles spatially, such that the various provinces of human civilization were brought up to the level of its most advanced outposts, and of forcing those societies in Europe and North America at the vanguard of civilization to implement their liberalism more fully.

[32] [author's note]: Kojéve's best known work is his Introduction à la lecture de Hegel (Paris: Editions Gallimard, 1947), which is a transcript of the Ecole Practique lectures from the 1930's. This book is available in English entitled *Introduction to the Reading of Hegel* arranged by Raymond Queneau, edited by Allan Bloom, and translated by James Nichols (New York: Basic Books, 1969).
[33] luminary: person of brilliant achievement
[34] imminent: about to happen
[35] to reject: to not accept
[36] latter: the last in a series
[37] [author's note]: In this respect Kojéve stands in sharp contrast to contemporary German interpreters of Hegel like Herbert Marcuse who, being more sympathetic to Marx, regarded Hegel ultimately as an historically bound and incomplete philosopher.
[38] the franchise: the right to vote
[39] attendant: accompanying

The state that emerges at the end of history is liberal insofar as it recognizes and protects through a system of law man's universal right to freedom, and democratic insofar as it exists only with the consent[40] of the governed. For Kojéve, this so-called "universal homogenous state" found real-life embodiment[41] in the countries of postwar Western Europe – precisely those flabby,[42] prosperous,[43] self-satisfied,[44] inward-looking, weak-willed states whose grandest project was nothing more heroic than the creation of the Common Market.[45] But this was only to be expected. For human history and the conflict that characterized it was based on the existence of "contradictions:" primitive man's quest for mutual recognition, the dialectic of the master and slave, the transformation and mastery of nature, the struggle for the universal recognition of rights, and the dichotomy[46] between proletarian and capitalist. But in the universal homogenous state, all prior contradictions are resolved and all human needs are satisfied. There is no struggle or conflict over "large" issues, and consequently no need for generals or statesmen; what remains is primarily economic activity. And indeed, Kojéve's life was consistent with his teaching. Believing that there was no more work for philosophers as well, since Hegel (correctly understood) had already achieved absolute knowledge, Kojéve left teaching after the war and spent the remainder[47] of his life working as a bureaucrat in the European Economic Community, until his death in 1968.

To his contemporaries[48] at mid-century, Kojéve's proclamation[49] of the end of history must have seemed like the typical eccentric solipsism[50] of a French intellectual, coming as it did on the heels of[51] World War II and at the very height of the Cold War. To comprehend how Kojéve could

---

[40] consent: agreement
[41] embodiment: the physical representation of an abstract thing
[42] flabby: weak
[43] prosperous: economically successful
[44] self-satisfied: overly pleased with one's condition
[45] [author's note]: Kojéve alternatively identified the end of history with the postwar "American way of life," toward which he thought the Soviet Union was moving as well.
[46] dichotomy: a division into two groups which seem in conflict
[47] remainder: rest
[48] contemporary: s.o. living at the same time
[49] proclamation: announcement
[50] solipsism: the belief that one's self is the only thing which exists
[51] on the heels of: immediately after s.th.

have been so audacious[52] as to assert that history has ended, we must first of all understand the meaning of Hegelian idealism.

II

For Hegel, the contradictions that drive history exist first of all in the realm of human consciousness, i.e. on the level of ideas[53] – not the trivial[54] election year proposals of American politicians, but ideas in the sense of large unifying world views that might best be understood under the rubric of ideology. Ideology in this sense is not restricted to the secular and explicit political doctrines we usually associate with the term, but can include religion, culture, and the complex of moral values underlying any society as well.

Hegel's view of the relationship between the ideal and the real or material worlds was an extremely complicated one, beginning with the fact that for him the distinction between the two was only apparent.[55] He did not believe that the real world conformed or could be made to conform to ideological preconceptions of philosophy professors in any simple-minded way, or that the "material" world could not impinge on[56] the ideal. Indeed, Hegel the professor was temporarily thrown out of work as a result of a very material event, the Battle of Jena. But while Hegel's writing and thinking could be stopped by a bullet from the material world, the hand on the trigger of the gun was motivated in turn by the ideas of liberty and equality that had driven the French Revolution.

For Hegel, all human behavior in the material world, and hence all human history, is rooted in a prior state of consciousness – an idea similar to the one expressed by John Maynard Keynes[57] when he said that the

52 audacious: bold
53 [author's note]: This notion was expressed in the famous aphorism from the preface to the *Philosophy of History* to the effect that "everything that is rational is real, and everything that is real is rational."
54 trivial: of little importance
55 [author's note]: Indeed, for Hegel the very dichotomy between the ideal and material worlds was itself only an apparent one that was ultimately overcome by the self-conscious subject; in his system, the material world is itself only an aspect of mind.
56 to impinge on [ɪmˈpɪndʒ]: to have an effect on s.th.
57 John Maynard Keynes [keɪnz] (1883–1946): British economist of international influence

views of men of affairs[58] were usually derived from defunct[59] economists and academic scribblers of earlier generations. This consciousness may not be explicit and self-aware, as are modern political doctrines, but may rather take the form of religion or simple cultural or moral habits. And yet this realm[60] of consciousness in the long run necessarily becomes manifest in the material world, indeed creates the material world in its own image. Consciousness is cause and not effect, and can develop autonomously from the material world; hence the real subtext underlying the apparent jumble[61] of current events is the history of ideology.

Hegel's idealism has fared[62] poorly at the hands of later thinkers. Marx reversed the priority of the real and the ideal completely, relegating[63] the entire realm of consciousness – religion, art, culture, philosophy itself – to a "superstructure" that was determined entirely by the prevailing material mode[64] of production. Yet another unfortunate legacy[65] of Marxism is our tendency to retreat into materialist or utilitarian explanations of political or historical phenomena, and our disinclination[66] to believe in the autonomous power of ideas. A recent example of this is Paul Kennedy's hugely successful *The Rise and Fall of the Great Powers*, which ascribes[67] the decline of great powers to simple economic overextension.[68] Obviously, this is true on some level: an empire whose economy is barely above the level of subsistence[69] cannot bankrupt its treasury indefinitely.[70] But whether a highly productive modern industrial society chooses to spend 3 or 7 percent of its GNP[71] on defense rather than consumption is entirely a matter of that society's political priorities, which are in turn determined in the realm of consciousness.

---

58 men of affairs: businessmen
59 defunct: no longer functioning
60 realm [relm]: area
61 jumble: confusion
62 to fare: to get along
63 to relegate: to give s.th. or s.o. a less important position
64 mode: method
65 legacy: something passed down from an earlier generation
66 disinclination: lack of enthusiasm for s.th.
67 to ascribe: to attribute
68 economic overextension: spending more money than you can afford
69 subsistence: survival
70 indefinitely: without a time limit
71 GNP: gross national product; the total value of all the goods and services produced by a country in one year

[...]

The materialist bias of modern thought is characteristic not only of people on the Left who may be sympathetic to Marxism, but of many passionate anti-Marxists as well. Indeed, there is on the Right what one might label the *Wall Street Journal* school of deterministic materialism that discounts[72] the importance of ideology and culture and sees man as essentially a rational, profit-maximizing individual. It is precisely this kind of individual and his pursuit of material incentives that is posited[73] as the basis for economic life as such in economic textbooks.[74] One small example will illustrate the problematic character of such materialist views.

Max Weber begins his famous book, *The Protestant Ethic and the Spirit of Capitalism*, by noting the different economic performance of Protestant and Catholic communities throughout Europe and America, summed up in the proverb[75] that Protestants eat well while Catholics sleep well. Weber notes that according to any economic theory that posited man as a rational profit-maximizer, raising the piece-work rate should increase labor productivity. But in fact, in many traditional peasant communities, raising the piece-work rate actually had the opposite effect of *lowering* labor productivity: at the higher rate, a peasant accustomed to earning two and one-half marks per day found he could earn the same amount by working less, and did so because he valued leisure more than income. The choices of leisure over income, or of the militaristic life of the Spartan hoplite[76] over the wealth of the Athenian trader, or even the ascetic life of the early capitalist entrepreneur over that of a traditional leisured aristocrat, cannot possibly be explained by the impersonal working of material forces, but come preeminently[77] out of the sphere of consciousness – what we have labeled here broadly as ideology. And indeed, a central theme of Weber's work was to prove that contrary

[72] to discount: to dismiss, to think s.th. is not important or not true

[73] to posit: to postulate

[74] [author's note] In fact, modern economists, recognizing that man does not always behave as a *profit*-maximizer, posit a "utility" function, utility being either income or some other good that can be maximized: leisure, sexual satisfaction, or the pleasure of philosophizing. That profit must be replaced with a value like utility indicates the cogency of the idealist perspective.

[75] proverb: wise saying

[76] hoplite (ancient Greece): a citizen-soldier

[77] preeminently: mainly

to Marx, the material mode of production, far from being the "base," was itself a "superstructure" with roots in religion and culture, and that to understand the emergence of modern capitalism and the profit motive one had to study their antecedents[78] in the realm of the spirit.

As we look around the contemporary world, the poverty of materialist theories of economic development is all too apparent. The *Wall Street Journal* school of deterministic materialism habitually points to the stunning economic success of Asia in the past few decades as evidence of the viability of free market economics, with the implication that all societies would see similar development were they simply to allow their populations to pursue their material self-interest freely. Surely free markets and stable political systems are a necessary precondition to capitalist economic growth. But just as surely the cultural heritage of those Far Eastern societies, the ethic of work and saving and family, a religious heritage that does not, like Islam, place restrictions on certain forms of economic behavior, and other deeply ingrained[79] moral qualities, are equally important in explaining their economic performance.[80] And yet the intellectual weight of materialism is such that not a single respectable contemporary theory of economic development addresses consciousness and culture seriously as the matrix[81] within which economic behavior is formed.

Failure to understand that the roots of economic behavior lie in the realm of consciousness and culture leads to the common mistake of attributing[82] material causes to phenomena that are essentially ideal in nature. For example, it is commonplace in the West to interpret the reform movements first in China and most recently in the Soviet Union as the victory of the material over the ideal – that is, a recognition that ideological incentives could not replace material ones in stimulating a highly productive modern economy, and that if one wanted to prosper one had

---

[78] antecedent: what came before

[79] ingrained: deep-rooted

[80] [author's note] One need look no further than the recent performance of Vietnamese immigrants in the U.S. school system when compared to their black of Hispanic classmates to realize that culture and consciousness are absolutely crucial to explain not only economic behavior but virtually every other important aspect of life as well.

[81] matrix: structure, basis, framework

[82] to attribute: to believe s.th. is the cause or responsible for s.th.

to appeal to baser[83] forms of self-interest. But the deep defects of socialist economies were evident thirty or forty years ago to anyone who chose to look. Why was it that these countries moved away from central planning only in the 1980s'? The answer must be found in the consciousness of the elites and leaders ruling them, who decided to opt for[84] the "Protestant" life of wealth and risk over the "Catholic" path of poverty and security.[85] That change was in no way made inevitable by the material conditions in which either country found itself on the eve of[86] the reform, but instead came about as the result of the victory of one idea over another.[87]

For Kojéve, as for all good Hegelians, understanding the underlying processes of history requires understanding developments in the realm of consciousness or ideas, since consciousness will ultimately remake the material world in its own image. To say that history ended in 1806 meant that mankind's ideological evolution ended in the ideals of the French or American Revolutions: while particular regimes in the real world might not implement[88] these ideals fully, their theoretical truth is absolute and could not be improved upon. Hence it did not matter to Kojéve that the consciousness of the postwar generation of Europeans had not been universalized throughout the world; if ideological development had in fact ended, the homogenous state would eventually become victorious throughout the material world.

[...]

I have neither the space nor, frankly, the ability to defend in depth Hegel's radical idealist perspective. The issue is not whether Hegel's system was right, but whether his perspective might uncover the problematic nature of many materialist explanations we often take for granted. This is not

---

[83] baser: less noble

[84] to opt for: to choose to take or not to take a certain course of action

[85] [author's note] I understand that a full explanation of the origins of the reform movements in China and Russia is a good deal more complicated than this simple formula would suggest. The Soviet reform, for example, was motivated in good measure by Moscow's sense of insecurity in the technological-military realm. Nonetheless, neither country on the eve of its reforms was in such a state of material crisis that one could have predicted the surprising reform paths ultimately taken.

[86] on the eve of (fig.): immediately before

[87] [author's note] It is still not clear whether the Soviet people are as "Protestant" as Gorbachev [in 1989] and will follow him down that path.

[88] to implement: to make use of s.th.

FREEDOM HOUSE

M

FREEDOM HOUSE

Survey Findings

Freedom Status	Country Breakdown	Population Breakdown (in billions)
FREE	90 (47%)	3.03 (46%)
PARTLY FREE	60 (31%)	1.19 (18%)
NOT FREE	43 (22%)	2.39 (36%)
TOTAL	**193 (100%)**	**6.61 (100%)**

p of Freedom 2008

The Map of Freedom reflects the findings of Freedom ouse's *Freedom in the World 2008* survey, which tes the level of political rights and civil liberties in 93 countries and 15 related and disputed territories uring 2007. Based on these ratings, countries are vided into three categories: **Free**, **Partly Free**, and **ot Free**.

A Free country is one where there is broad scope for open political competition, a climate of respect for civil liberties, significant independent civic life, and independent media.

Partly Free countries are characterized by some restrictions on political rights and civil liberties, often in a context of corruption, weak rule of law, ethnic strife, or civil war.

A Not Free country is one where basic political rights are absent, and basic civil liberties are widely and systematically denied.

Freedom House is an independent nongovernmental organization that supports the expansion of freedom worldwide.

www.freedomhouse.org

to deny the role of material factors as such. To a literal-minded[89] idealist, human society can be built around any arbitrary set of principles regardless of their relationship to the material world. And in fact men have proven themselves able to endure[90] the most extreme material hardships in the name of ideas that exist in the realm of the spirit alone, be it the divinity[91] of cows or the nature of the Holy Trinity.[92]

But while man's very perception of the material world is shaped by his historical consciousness of it, the material world can clearly affect in return the viability of a particular state of consciousness. In particular, the spectacular abundance of advanced liberal economies and the infinitely diverse consumer culture made possible by them seem to both foster[93] and preserve liberalism in the political sphere. I want to avoid the materialist determinism that says that liberal economics inevitably produces liberal politics, because I believe that both economics and politics presuppose an autonomous prior state of consciousness that makes them possible. But that state of consciousness that permits the growth of liberalism seems to stabilize in the way one would expect at the end of history if it is underwritten[94] by the abundance of a modern free market economy. We might summarize the content of the universal homogenous state as liberal democracy in the political sphere combined with easy access to VCRs[95] and stereos in the economic.

[89] literal-minded: following the narrow definition
[90] to endure: to suffer
[91] divinity: god-like quality
[92] [author's note] The internal politics of the Byzantine Empire at the time of Justinian revolved around a conflict between the so-called monophysites and monothelites, who believed that the unity of the Holy Trinity was alternatively one of nature or of will. This conflict corresponded to some extent to one between proponents of different racing teams in the Hippodrome in Byzantium and led to a not insignificant level of political violence. Modern historians would tend to seek the roots of such conflicts in antagonisms between social classes or some other modern economic category, being unwilling to believe that men would kill each other over the nature of the Trinity.
[93] to foster: to promote
[94] to underwrite: to guarantee
[95] VCR: video cassette recorder

III

Have we in fact reached the end of history? Are there, in other words, any fundamental "contradictions" in human life that cannot be resolved in the context of modern liberalism, that would be resolvable by an alternative political-economic structure? If we accept the idealist premises laid out above, we must seek an answer to this question in the realm of ideology and consciousness. Our task is not to answer exhaustively the challenges to liberalism promoted by every crackpot[96] messiah around the world, but only those that are embodied[97] in important social or political forces and movements, and which are therefore part of world history. For our purposes, it matters very little what strange thoughts occur to people in Albania or Burkina Faso,[98] for we are interested in what one could in some sense call the common ideological heritage of mankind.

In the past century, there have been two major challenges to liberalism, those of fascism and of communism. The former[99] saw the political weakness, materialism, anomie,[100] and lack of community of the West as fundamental contradictions in liberal societies that could only be resolved by a strong state that forged[101] a new "people" on the basis of national exclusiveness. Fascism was destroyed as a living ideology by World War II. This was a defeat, of course, on a very material level, but it amounted to a defeat of the idea as well. What destroyed fascism as an idea was not universal moral revulsion[102] against it, since plenty of people were willing to endorse[103] the idea as long as it seemed the wave of the future, but

[96] crackpot (slang): crazy

[97] to embody: to include or contain

[98] Burkina Faso: country in west Africa

[99] [author's note] I am not using the term "fascism" here in its most precise sense, fully aware of the frequent misuse of this term to denounce anyone to the right of the user. "Fascism" here denotes nay organized ultra nationalist movement with universalistic pretensions - not universalistic with regard to its nationalism, of course, since the latter is exclusive by definition, but with regard to the movement's belief in its right to rule other people. Hence Imperial Japan would qualify as fascist while former strongman Stoessner's Paraguay or Pinochet's Chile would not. Obviously fascist ideologies cannot be universalistic in the sense of Marxism or liberalism, but the structure of the doctrine can be transferred from country to country.

[100] anomie: social instability due to a decline in standards and values

[101] to forge: to form

[102] revulsion: strong dislike

[103] to endorse: to support

its lack of success. After the war, it seemed to most people that German fascism as well as its other European and Asian variants were bound[104] to self-destruct. There was no material reason why new fascist movements could not have sprung up again after the war in other locales,[105] but for the fact that expansionist ultranationalism, with its promise of unending conflict leading to disastrous military defeat, had completely lost its appeal.[106] The ruins of the Reich chancellery as well as the atomic bombs dropped on Hiroshima and Nagasaki killed this ideology on the level of consciousness as well as materially, and all of the pro-fascist movements spawned[107] by the German and Japanese examples like the Perónist[108] movement in Argentina or Subhas Chandra Bose's[109] Indian National Army withered[110] after the war.

The ideological challenge mounted[111] by the other great alternative to liberalism, communism, was far more serious. Marx, speaking Hegel's language, asserted that liberal society contained a fundamental contradiction that could not be resolved within its context, that between capital and labor, and this contradiction has constituted[112] the chief accusation[113] against liberalism ever since. But surely, the class issue has actually been successfully resolved in the West. As Kojéve (among others) noted, the egalitarianism of modern America represents the essential achievement of the classless society envisioned by Marx. This is not to say that there are not rich people and poor people in the United States, or that the gap between them has not grown in recent years. But the root causes of economic inequality do not have to do with the underlying legal and social structure of our society, which remains fundamentally egalitar-

---

[104] bound: destined
[105] locale [ləʊ'kɑ:l]: place
[106] appeal: attraction
[107] to spawn (fig.): to give life to s.th.
[108] Perónist: having to do with Juan Domingo Perón (1895–1974), military officer and politician who was elected as President of Argentina three times. Although thought by many to be a demagogue he attempted to eliminate poverty in his country.
[109] Subhas Chandra Bose (1897–1945?): Indian revolutionary who led an Indian national political and military force against Britain and the Western powers during World War II
[110] to wither: to die slowly
[111] to mount: to organize
[112] to constitute: to make up
[113] accusation: a charge of wrongdoing

ian and moderately redistributionist,[114] so much as with the cultural and social characteristics of the groups that make it up, which are in turn the historical legacy of premodern conditions. Thus black poverty in the United States is not the inherent[115] product of liberalism, but is rather the "legacy of slavery and racism" which persisted long after the formal abolition of slavery.

As a result of the receding[116] of the class issue, the appeal of communism in the developed Western world, it is safe to say, is lower today than any time since the end of the First World War. This can be measured in any number of ways: in the declining membership and electoral pull of the major European communist parties, and their overtly[117] revisionist[118] programs; in the corresponding electoral success of conservative parties from Britain and Germany to the United States and Japan, which are unabashedly pro-market and anti-statist;[119] and in an intellectual climate whose most "advanced" members no longer believe that bourgeois[120] society is something that ultimately needs to be overcome.

[...]

If we admit for the moment that the fascist and communist challenges to liberalism are dead, are there any other ideological competitors left? Or put another way, are there contradictions in liberal society beyond that of class that are not resolvable? Two possibilities suggest themselves, those of religion and nationalism.

The rise of religious fundamentalism in recent years within the Christian, Jewish, and Muslim traditions has been widely noted. One is inclined to say that the revival of religion in some way attests[121] to a broad unhappiness with the impersonality and spiritual vacuity[122] of liberal consumerist societies. Yet while the emptiness at the core of liberalism is

[114] redistributionist: taking from those who have more and giving it to those who have less
[115] inherent: resulting from its nature
[116] to recede: to disappear
[117] overtly: done in an open way, not secretly
[118] revisionist: moderate, non-revolutionary
[119] anti-statist: against government control of the economy
[120] bourgeois ['bʊəʒwɑː]: middle-class
[121] to attest: to offer proof
[122] vacuity: emptiness

most certainly a defect in the ideology [...] it is not at all clear that it is remediable[123] through politics. Modern liberalism itself was historically a consequence of the weakness of religiously-based societies which, failing to agree on the nature of the good life, could not provide even the minimal preconditions of peace and stability. In the contemporary world only Islam has offered a theocratic state as a political alternative to both liberalism and communism. But the doctrine has little appeal for non-Muslims, and it is hard to believe that the movement will take on any universal significance. Other less organized religious impulses have been successfully satisfied within the sphere of personal life that is permitted in liberal societies.

The other major "contradiction" potentially unresolvable by liberalism is the one posed by nationalism and other forms of racial and ethnic consciousness. [...] Two cataclysmic[124] world wars in this century have been spawned by the nationalism of the developed world in various guises,[125] and if those passions have been muted[126] to a certain extent in postwar Europe, they are still extremely powerful in the Third World. Nationalism has been a threat to liberalism historically in Germany, and continues to be one in isolated parts of "post-historical" Europe like Northern Ireland.

But it is not clear that nationalism represents an irreconcilable[127] contradiction in the heart of liberalism. In the first place, nationalism is not one single phenomenon but several, ranging from mild cultural nostalgia to the highly organized and elaborately[128] articulated doctrine of National Socialism. Only systematic nationalisms of the latter sort can qualify as a formal ideology on the level of liberalism or communism. The vast majority of the world's nationalist movements do not have a political program beyond the negative desire of independence from some other group or people, and do not offer anything like a comprehensive[129] agenda for socio-economic organization. As such, they are compatible with doctrines and ideologies that do offer such agendas. While they may

---

123 remediable [rɪˈmiːdiəbl]: that can be solved
124 cataclysmic [ˌkætəˈklɪzmɪk]: catastrophic
125 guise [gaɪz]: form
126 to mute [mjuːt]: to tone down
127 irreconcilable [ˌɪrˌeknˈsaɪləbl]: with no possible solution because the differences are too great
128 elaborately: with great detail
129 comprehensive: complete, full, containing almost all details

constitute a source of conflict for liberal societies, this conflict does not arise from liberalism itself so much as from the fact that the liberalism in question is incomplete. Certainly a great deal of the world's ethnic and nationalist tension can be explained in terms of peoples who are forced to live in unrepresentative political systems that they have not chosen.

While it is impossible to rule out[130] the sudden appearance of new ideologies or previously unrecognized contradictions in liberal societies, then, the present world seems to confirm that the fundamental principles of sociopolitical organization have not advanced terribly far since 1806. Many of the wars and revolutions fought since that time have been undertaken in the name of ideologies which claimed to be more advanced than liberalism, but whose pretensions[131] were ultimately unmasked[132] by history. In the meantime, they have helped to spread the universal homogenous state to the point where it could have a significant effect on the overall character of international relations.

IV

[...]

The expansionist and competitive behavior of nineteenth-century European states rested on no less ideal a basis; it just so happened that the ideology driving it was less explicit than the doctrines of the twentieth century. For one thing, most "liberal" European societies were illiberal insofar as they believed in the legitimacy of imperialism, that is, the right of one nation to rule over other nations without regard for the wishes of the ruled. The justifications for imperialism varied from nation to nation, from a crude belief in the legitimacy of force, particularly when applied to non-Europeans, to the White Man's Burden[133] and Europe's Christianizing mission, to the desire to give people of color access to the culture of Rabelais[134] and Molière.[135] But whatever the particular ideo-

[130] to rule out: to exclude
[131] pretension: claim (*Behauptung*)
[132] to unmask: to expose
[133] White man's burden: controversial title of a poem by Rudyard Kipling, which claims that whites have a duty to civilize the rest of the world
[134] François Rabelais ['ræbəleɪ] (c. 1494–1553): major French Renaissance writer
[135] Jean-Baptiste Poquelin, stage name Molière ['mɒlieə] (1622–1673): major French playwright and actor

logical basis, every "developed" country believed in the acceptability of higher civilizations ruling lower ones – including, incidentally,[136] the United States with regard to the Philippines. This led to a drive for pure territorial aggrandizement[137] in the latter half of the century and played no small role in causing the Great War.[138]

The radical and deformed[139] outgrowth of nineteenth-century imperialism was German fascism, an ideology which justified Germany's right not only to rule over non-European peoples, but over all non-German ones. But in retrospect[140] it seems that Hitler represented a diseased bypath[141] in the general course of European development, and since his fiery[142] defeat, the legitimacy of any kind of territorial aggrandizement has been thoroughly discredited.[143] Since the Second World War, European nationalism has been defanged[144] and shorn of[145] any real relevance to foreign policy, with the consequence that the nineteenth-century model of great power behavior has become a serious anachronism. The most extreme form of nationalism that any Western European state has mustered[146] since 1945 has been Gaullism,[147] whose self-assertion has been confined largely to the realm of nuisance[148] politics and culture. International life for the part of the world that has reached the end of history is far more preoccupied with economics than with politics or strategy.

[...]

---

136 incidentally: interjection meaning "by the way"
137 aggrandizement: expansion
138 the Great War: the First World War
139 to deform: to distort
140 retrospect: a review of past events
141 bypath: a little traveled side path
142 fiery ['faɪəri]: consisting of fire
143 [author's note] It took European colonial powers like France several years after the war to admit the illegitimacy of their empires, but decolonialization was an inevitable consequence of the Allied victory which had been based on the promise of a restoration of democratic freedoms.
144 to defang (fig.): to make less powerful
145 to be shorn of (fig.): to be stripped of s.th., to have s.th. removed or taken away
146 to muster: to summon, to gather
147 Gaullism: relating to the policies of Charles de Gaulle (1890–1970), a former President of France
148 nuisance ['nju:sns]: s.th. causing annoyance

V

The passing of Marxism-Leninism first from China and then from the Soviet Union will mean its death as a living ideology of world historical significance. For while there may be some isolated true believers left in places like Managua,[149] Pyongyang,[150] or Cambridge, Massachusetts,[151] the fact that there is not a single large state in which it is a going concern undermines completely its pretensions to being in the vanguard of human history. And the death of this ideology means the growing "Common Marketization" of international relations, and the diminution[152] of the likelihood of large-scale conflict between states.

This does not by any means imply the end of international conflict per se.[153] For the world at that point would be divided between a part that was historical and a part that was post-historical. Conflict between states is still in history, and between those states and those at the end of history, would still be possible. There would still be a high and perhaps rising level of ethnic and nationalist violence, since those are impulses incompletely played out, even in parts of the post-historical world. Palestinians and Kurds, Sikhs and Tamils, Irish Catholics and Walloons, Armenians and Azeris, will continue to have their unresolved grievances.[154] This implies that terrorism and wars of national liberation will continue to be an important item on the international agenda. But large-scale conflict must involve large states still caught in the grip of history, and they are what appear to be passing from the scene.

[...]

149 Managua: capital of Nicaragua – At the time of this article Nicaragua had a marxist government.
150 Pyongyang: capital of communist North Korea
151 Cambridge, Massachusetts: city containing Harvard University and MIT (Massachusetts Institute of Technology), i.e. a city containing a large body of liberal intellectuals
152 diminution: decrease
153 per se (Latin): in itself
154 grievance: complaint

Joseph E. Stiglitz was born in Gary, Indiana in 1943. He received a BA from Amherst College and his Ph.D. from MIT. He was awarded the John Bates Clark Award, given biennially by the American Economic Association to the economist under 40 who has made the most significant contribution to the field. In 2001, he was awarded the Nobel Prize in economics, and he was a lead author of the 1995 *Report of the Intergovernmental Panel on Climate Change*, which shared the 2007 Nobel Peace Prize. Stiglitz was a member of the Council of Economic Advisers during the Clinton administration and later became Chief Economist and Senior Vice-President of the World Bank. Recognized around the globe as a leading economic educator, he has written textbooks that have been translated into more than a dozen languages. His book *Globalization and Its Discontents* has been translated into 35 languages and has sold more than one million copies worldwide. He is currently a Professor at Columbia University and lives with his wife in New York.

In the excerpt below, Stiglitz emphasizes that the real question for our time is not if one is for or against globalization, but how the global system should be constructed. He argues that one of the main principles of it must be uniformity, or fairness, otherwise it will merely be a guise[1] for the abuse of power and privilege. Although one of the most prominent critics of how globalization has developed, he too is optimistic that it will bring about positive changes in the lives of millions of people around the world.

You can watch a lecture by Joseph Stiglitz at: http://www.youtube.com/watch?v=UzhD7KVs-R4.

---

[1] guise [gaɪz]: (here): system or method whose real purpose is hidden

Making Globalization Work[2]

by Joseph E. Stiglitz

Is reform possible?

I have been pleased with the reception that this book has received. The rapid translation of the book into twenty-one languages afforded me the opportunity to engage in a global debate about globalization. My first book, *Globalization and Its Discontents*, helped shift the debate away from a simplistic one of whether one was for or against globalization. The question was, rather, how globalization was managed. *Making Globalization Work*, too, has helped shift the debate. Today, few deny the problem of growing inequality, to which globalization has contributed. No one really thinks the world is flat. Today, the debate has shifted to the merits[3] of particular reform measures.

But a question I have repeatedly been asked is why I am optimistic that there will be any significant reforms – at least in the right direction. Friendly critics say that I have pointed out clearly the failures in globalization and the political forces which have given rise to those problems. Why, they ask, would a lecture – or a book – change anything? It is not likely that American cotton producers, having heard the harm that cotton subsidies[4] cause poor farmers in Africa or elsewhere, or hearing the stories of the Indian cotton farmers, who are depressed by their inability to meet their debt obligations as a result of low prices caused in part by America's cotton subsidies and who are being driven to commit suicide, will say: "Thank you for telling us. We were only trying to help ourselves. We meant no harm to others. Now that we realize all this, we will ask Congress to repeal the subsidies." I have always been impressed with the ability of individuals to rationalize what makes them better off with their sense of ethics and their economic beliefs. Those who otherwise believe in free markets – and argue against welfare payments to the poor because of the effect it has in weakening incentives – nonetheless are more than willing to accept, even demand, subsidies for themselves.

---

[2] Joseph E. Stiglitz, *Making Globalization Work*, New York: W. W. Norton and Company, 2007, 305–306.

[3] merit: positive quality

[4] subsidy: financial support provided by the government

"You ever get the feeling that this economy benefits some people more than others?"

I agree with the critics that a book such as mine – or ten books like it – by itself will not lead to a revolutionary reform of globalization. But there are changes at play in the global economy – the increasing global imbalances, the mounting evidence on global warming, the continuing stalemate[5] in the development round trade talks, the growing dissatisfaction with the World Bank, the rising awareness of the dangers of unilateralism,[6] the WTO[7] decision that America's cotton subsidies are "illegal" – which, inevitably, will change the way globalization is managed.

---

[5] stalemate: a situation in which opponents see no possibility for further action

[6] unilateralism: a foreign policy whereby a nation deals with foreign affairs alone without considering the wishes of other countries

[7] WTO: World Trade Organization, an organization that deals with the regulation of trade between participating countries

My hope is that this book will help nudge[8] the changes in the right direction.

[8] to nudge: to push slightly

Recommended Reading

Noam Chomsky

Hopes and Prospects, Chicago: Haymarket Books, 2010

Tyler Cowen

Creative Destruction: How Globalization Is Changing the World's Cultures, Princeton: Princeton University Press, 2002

Richard Florida

Who's Your City?: How the Creative Economy Is Making Where to Live the Most Important Decision of Your Life, New York: Basic Books, 2009

The Rise of the Creative Class, New York: Basic Books, 2003

Thomas L. Friedman

Hot, Flat, and Crowded 2.0: Why We Need a Green Revolution – and How It Can Renew America, London: Picador, 2009

The World Is Flat 3.0: A Brief History of the Twenty-first Century, London: Picador, 2007

Francis Fukuyama

The Origins of Political Order: From Prehuman Times to the French Revolution, New York: Farrar, Straus and Giroux, 2011

The End of History and the Last Man, New York: Avon, 2006

Al Gore

Our Choice: A Plan to Solve the Climate Crisis, New York: Rodale Books, 2009

An Inconvenient Truth: The Planetary Emergency of Global Warming and What We Can Do About It, New York: Rodale Books, 2006

Bruce C. N. Greenwald and Judd Kahn

Globalization: The Irrational Fear That Someone in China Will Take Your Job, Hoboken, NJ: John Wiley & Sons, 2009

Joseph S. Nye Jr.
The Future of Power, New York: Public Affairs, 2011

Jan Nederveen Pieterse
Globalization and Culture: Global Mélange, Lanham, MD: Rowman & Littlefield, 2009

Steven Pinker
The Better Angels of Our Nature: Why Violence Has Declined, New York: Viking, 2011

Clyde Prestowitz
Three Billion New Capitalists, New York: Basic Books, 2006

Joseph E. Stiglitz
Making Globalization Work, New York: W.W. Norton, 2007

Globalization and Its Discontents, New York: W.W. Norton, 2003

Muhammad Yunus
Building Social Business: The New Kind of Capitalism That Serves Humanity's Most Pressing Needs, New York: Public Affairs, 2010

Creating a World Without Poverty: Social Business and the Future of Capitalism, New York: Public Affairs, 2007

Banker To The Poor: Micro-Lending and the Battle Against World Poverty, New York: Public Affairs, 2003

Fareed Zakaria
The Post-American World: Release 2.0, New York: W.W. Norton, 2011

Picture references:

p. 10:	Getty Images / Soul Brother
p. 51:	John Morris © www.CartoonStock.com reprinted with permission
p. 88:	EPA / Justin Lane
p. 92:	© Mike Keefe, The Denver Post and InToon.com reprinted with permission
p. 105:	Getty Images / Matt Carr
p. 110:	© 2006 reprinted with the permission of Randy Glasbergen
p. 116:	Corbis / ZUMA Press / Ron Bull
p. 118:	Andrea Naumann, Aachen
p. 133:	dpa / picture-alliance
p. 144/145:	www.freedomhouse.org
p. 154:	Getty Images / Stephen Lovekin
p. 156:	Andrew Toos © www.CartoonStock.com used with permission